DU

How to Make Music on the Web

MICHAEL HEATLEY & ALAN KINSMAN

Get Online Fast
Expert Tips & Advice
Record ☆ Network ☆ Promote

Foreword by Ronan Macdonald

Publisher and Creative Director: Nick Wells
Project Editor: Sara Robson
Picture Research: Victoria Lyle
Art Director and Layout Design: Mike Spender
Digital Design and Production: Chris Herbert

Special thanks to Georgina Heatley, Petra Jones, Rebecca Kidd, Polly Prior and Julia Rolf

First published 2009 by
FLAME TREE PUBLISHING
Crabtree Hall, Crabtree Lane
Fulham, London SW6 6TY
United Kingdom

www.flametreepublishing.com
Music information site: www.musicfirebox.com

Flame Tree is part of the Foundry Creative Media Company Ltd
© 2009 The Foundry

09 11 13 12 10
1 3 5 7 9 10 8 6 4 2

Every effort has been made to contact copyright holders. We apologize in advance
for any omissions and would be pleased to insert the appropriate acknowledgement
in subsequent editions of this publication.

The CIP record for this book is available from the British Library.

ISBN: 978-1-84786-524-3

Printed in India

Contents

HOME RECORDING 74–175

Start Here

I want to write/perform great songs

Do you feel the burning desire to write heartfelt lyrics and perform your music live?

☆ Go to page 33 to learn how to structure your songs and how the Internet can help with those tricky rhymes.

☆ Go to page 53 for valuable tips on soundchecking in order to get your sound right for your gigs.

I want to record my music at home

Do you need to know what equipment and technology you need to make music at home?

☆ Go to page 108 to start learning about all the essential gear needed for home recording.

☆ Go to page 146 if you want to incorporate samples in your music – you can go to online sample banks!

I want to promote/distribute my music

Do you want to be proactive and make sure you are doing everything you can to get your music heard?

☆ Go to page 179 for how best to exploit social networking and video sites like MySpace, YouTube and Bebo.

☆ Go to page 215 if you are more ambitious and want to create your own website – each step is covered.

☆ Go to page 271 to start learning the various ways you can upload and distribute your music on the web.

☆ Go to page 354 for resources that can help you find managers, producers and labels – anyone who may become a part of your future success.

Foreword

Of all the creative arts, music has undoubtedly been the most affected by the unstoppable rise of the home computer. In fact, the word 'affected' doesn't even begin to do justice to what's happened – there's nothing short of a revolution going on in music today, and it's all thanks to the not-so-humble silicon chip. From production through promotion, distribution and even live performance, every stage of the modern musical process is dominated by software technology and – increasingly – the Internet.

Today, anyone with a Mac or PC can produce complete tracks in the comfort of their own home to an incredibly high standard, without being able to play so much as a note on an actual instrument. The divide between the home studio and the professional facility is getting narrower by the year, as consumer-priced software replaces expensive hardware in the latter and exponentially increases the power and output quality of the former.

Once you've made a track that you reckon the world deserves to hear, you certainly don't need a record or publishing deal to get it 'out there' – those days, too, are long gone. The record industry might have been sent into a tailspin by the Pandora's box of online distribution, but for the independent artist, it's nothing but good news. The net plays host to countless independent websites and communities that exist in large part to democratize music and give anyone who wants it the opportunity to expose their tunes. From social networking sites to online 'record' stores and radio stations, endless marketing possibilities and outlets are open to you as a music producer, no matter what genre you work in. The web has become the de facto home of the truly cutting-edge music listener – the listener who refuses to

be spoonfed commercial playlists; the listener who demands real choice without a primarily commercial agenda; the listener who might just be waiting to hear that song you've poured your heart and soul into.

Not so long ago, it took more money, time and specialist access to get a CD recorded, marketed and released than the home musician could even dream of. Now, lack of money is no obstacle, the CD is all but dead, and in a weekend, you – entirely on your own – can produce a track, put it online and promote the hell out of it. Who knows, you might even sell a few downloads and make a bit of money. Ain't that a thing?

Ronan Macdonald

Introduction

When the story of popular music is finally written, the single most influential invention in its history will be ... what? The electric guitar? The synthesizer? The drum kit? No, it's likely that the Internet will take pride of place. Because it's not only changed the way many of us consume music, but it has also provided a two-way highway for music to be bought and sold. We can obtain it in digital form from download sites or as CDs bought from virtual record shops and delivered to our door.

But if you are a musician the Internet also offers an exciting and seemingly limitless pool of opportunity. You can find like-minded musicians, advertise your band, create a mailing list of fans, invite their comments, let them hear your music and host videos showing yourselves in action. We show you how to make a website and the best way to use it. Creating music is also so much easier now: digital music files can be sent between songwriters and musicians, augmented and passed on. Not only do you no longer need a studio, you don't even have to be on the same continent! Computer software can be downloaded for home studio use, while advice and discussion websites help everyone take part in this revolution in music creation.

New opportunities are presenting themselves every day. Some have likened it to the do-it-yourself punk movement of the late 1970s, when bands pressed up their own records and sold them direct. But this is a tidal wave by comparison. You can have a fan on a South Sea Island who's never seen you in the flesh but can watch you and buy your music with the click of a mouse!

If you want management and/or a record label, then again the Internet is your friend. And if you want to get a fan following, the World Wide Web is the ideal medium. Using established social networking sites like MySpace, Facebook and Bebo to contact them and keep them informed has never been easier – we tell you how.

Though the impact of the online revolution is a long way from being fully realized, the reverberations have already been felt from the small to the mighty. Radiohead, for

instance, concentrated their promotional efforts for their 2000 album *Kid A* on the net with 30-second promo films called 'blips'. By *In Rainbows*, seven years later, they were selling music from their own website – and allowing purchasers to pay what they felt it was worth! That may be a step too far for you at the moment, but it does show that the age of the record company, like the record shop before it, is numbered. And, just as many of us have never bought a vinyl record, so the next generation will have to ask their parents what a CD is.

The digital revolution has reduced music to its purest form, cut out the middlemen and put the power in your hands. This book will help you take the first steps towards using it.

Michael Heatley

STARTING OUT

Even the greatest journey starts with a single step – and your first step to the stage can be a daunting prospect. Especially when it takes you via the rehearsal room, songwriting school and pounding the pavement getting gigs. This section will guide your footsteps, pointing the way to creating a show, finding an audience and keeping them. The talent and perseverance comes from you!

1
2
3
4
5
6
7
8
9
10
11
12

1

2

3

4

5

6

7

8

9

10

11

12

1

THE BASIC IDEA

Introduction

Even solo stars need a little help from their friends – so this section tells you how to find like-minded musicians, get your act together in rehearsal and prepare for your stage debut. It may seem a long way off right now, but once the project gathers pace you may find your momentum is unstoppable. The key is to stay focused, enjoy yourselves – remember, you're entertainers – and don't be afraid to be constructively critical. If you iron out the rough spots before the audience see or hear them, you'll be halfway to success.

1

Working With Others

Forming a band and joining a band are two different things. Joining an already existing group means conforming to their already established routines of rehearsing and performing. They will have a repertoire of songs you will have to learn in a style you (presumably) are happy to play. They may give you freedom to express yourself or (more likely) expect you to start by reproducing the contribution of the departed member. It's worth finding out why they parted ways so you can be aware of problems that might recur in future.

Finding a band that wants your services is best achieved by using one of the many 'musicians wanted' sites on the Internet. You an also use this to advertise for people

▶ *It can be difficult joining an existing band. Dave Navarro joined the Red Hot Chili Peppers in 1992 when John Frusciante left in the middle of a tour. However, he left a few years later due to creative differences.*

to form your own outfit. It's often easiest to get hold of one like-minded person first to form a nucleus with you – for instance, if you're a guitarist, look for a vocalist – and then you can 'add on' from there.

HANDY HINTS

Put yourself on websites as a 'musician available' as well as asking for other musicians to join you – that way you get two bites of the cherry.

▼ *Use sites such as www.joinmyband.co.uk to find a band or a musician.*

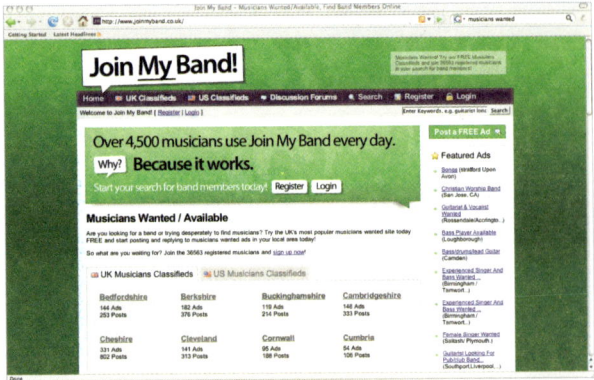

Advertising locally is another good idea. A postcard in your friendly local music shop is a good start, or ask around at school or college. You may find a cheap rehearsal facility there, too. But perhaps the best way of all is to find a local jam session in a pub, club or community centre. These are run weekly or monthly to create business on quiet nights, but you have the chance to see musicians in action before you make your move. Many excellent bands started from chance meetings at jams.

HANDY HINTS

When advertising for other musicians specify a wide range of influences, including bands you admire – vague terms tend to attract vague people.

▲ *Try advertising for new band members in your local music shop.*

1

2

3

4

5

6

7

8

9

10

11

12

▼ *Jam sessions give you the chance to see musicians in action before asking them to join your band.*

HANDY HINTS

Never let a lack of technical ability put you off forming or joining a band. It takes all sorts and, as Kurt Cobain and the Sex Pistols showed, attitude counts for a lot!

24

Improving Your Skills

Practice makes perfect is the oldest cliché in the book – and it's also very true. As with homework assignments, there are no short cuts; you get out what you put in.

Improving skills can be done in a general or specific way. Guitarists and bass players, for instance, have the luxury of being able to 'noodle' quietly while

▲ *Digital drum machines allow you to practise quietly, and many can record so that you can play back your rhythms.*

1

watching TV, and every minute that instrument is in your hands will make it more of a friend to you. Drummers have to set up a kit to practise – though many now use silent 'drum pads' at home. Singers can sing anywhere from the shower to the supermarket, though be prepared for complaints!

▲ *Singers can practice anywhere, from the shower to the supermarket.*

▼ *A digital audio recorder is an essential bit of kit for anyone looking to improve their playing.*

Specific practising means scales (singers and guitarists) or rudiments (drums) – the exercises that will give you the musical vocabulary to interact with others. Another kind of specific practising is to focus on songs – either playing/ singing along with a CD or the radio, or developing something you have created yourself.

The most effective way of improving your skills is to record or video yourself and work on your weaknesses. If you are your own toughest critic, you can make good progress. But don't let that be at the expense of your self-confidence: get a piece of paper and make a list of your strong points down one side and weaknesses on the other. Appreciate the former, work on the latter and you will be on the way to becoming an all-round entertainer.

Getting The Most Out Of Rehearsals

Rehearsals are where new material is introduced and where existing material is polished to a performance standard. Make sure you know which you want to do. There is nothing worse than turning up week after week and finding you're starting from scratch each time with a whole new set of songs you haven't tried before.

▼ *Take the time to make sure all of your equipment is in tip-top condition – your rehearsal time is better spent playing than fixing your gear.*

If a plan is agreed – and someone has to circulate one! – people can do their homework and turn up with their part already learned. That is, of course, if you're covering an existing song by someone else. If your songs are original, the writer can send demo sketches via the Internet so the individual musicians can think about their parts before getting together.

◄ *Make sure you know what you want to get out of your rehearsal. Are you experimenting with new material or polishing old songs?*

1

HANDY HINTS

Find a good place to rehearse and book it for the same night each week. This will force you to keep the momentum going and not let things drop.

Rehearsals may be informal affairs, but it's very easy to waste time. If you rehearse at home or a friend's place, move every fourth rehearsal you do to a studio. Not only does this make you aware that time is precious and should be used but it will probably give you more room to spread out and set up in the way you intend to on stage. That's important for visual cues before endings or breaks.

Obvious points: if a rehearsal is from, say, 6–10 p.m., does everyone turn up at six or can the drummer get there earlier to set up his kit?

▲ *Rehearsal time is precious. Don't be late!*

▼ *Do you know what equipment you need to bring to each rehearsal? For example, do you need to bring your own microphone? Make sure that you remember everything.*

Same for anyone else who needs set-up time. And who is responsible for the vocal (PA system)? Do they have all the mics or do people bring their own? Make sure everyone knows what's required: there's nothing more frustrating than sitting round watching the time tick away when you could be making music.

In short, have a plan, agree it, execute it and move forward towards your goal – live performance!

1

Songwriting Basics

Where to start? At the risk of sounding obvious, titles and opening lines are good points to work from. A strong first line is good to reel the listener in, but there has to be something somewhere in the three minutes that follow that will stay in the mind of the listener. This all-important hook can be vocal or instrumental.

▲ *It can be difficult to know where to begin when trying to write a song. A strong first line is a good place to start.*

▼ *Online rhyming dictionaries, such as www.rhymer.com, can help with difficult rhymes.*

Verses tend to be quieter than choruses, and this contrast helps to add interest to the whole song. The aim is get a natural sense of light and shade between verse and chorus.

Rhymes are needed to give the song a feeling of completion, while a middle eight after a couple of verses and choruses will pique the listener's imagination; just as they feel they have a handle on the song, it adds another element.

1

▼ *'Yesterday' was voted the best song of the twentieth century in a 1999 BBC Radio 2 poll of music experts and listeners.*

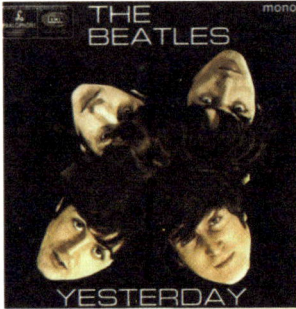

The song's chorus should arrive within a minute of the start – though rules are there to be broken. The Beatles' 'Yesterday' has no conventional chorus at all, while Abba's 'Take A Chance On Me' brazenly starts with the chorus. As for titles, we're still waiting for Kurt Cobain to sing the words 'Smells Like Teen Spirit'....

Your life may be full of song-worthy stories, but if not don't despair. Songwriters can find inspiration for subject matter from current events or even tabloid headlines. These are often eye-catchingly snappy, and can make great starting points for songs.

▶ *Read newspapers or go online to find out about current affairs, which can be great inspiration for songs.*

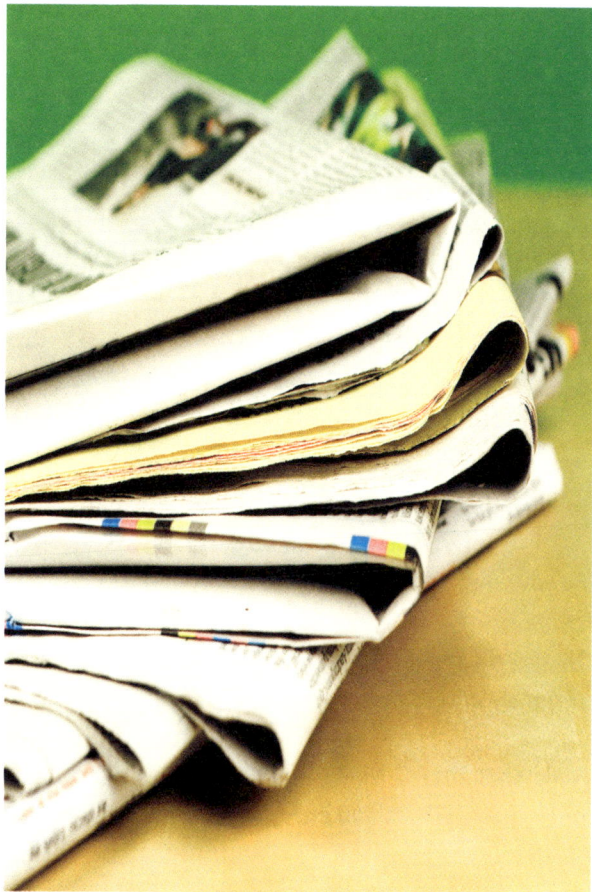

Finally, try to set yourself a target number of songs to write per month. Nine of the 10 may be thrown away but it's all part of the learning curve – the 10th could be your Grammy-winner!

Summary

Check your progress against this list

Use the Internet to advertise your
availability and/or find like-minded
musicians you can work with . . . . ☐

Never stop trying to improve your
vocal and instrumental skills . . . . ☐

Practise 'unplugged' if you have to, or invest
in headphones to keep the sound to yourself . . . ☐

Be your own critic – but don't lose confidence. . . ☐

Make sure everyone takes rehearsals
seriously and turns up on time . . . . ☐

Make sure there's a list of songs to work
on agreed upfront and encourage people
to 'do their homework' . . . . ☐

Analyse your favourite groups' songs
and try to learn from them . . . . ☐

Write as many songs as you can and
look for the 'diamond' . . . . ☐

1
2
3
4
5
6
7
8
9
10
11
12

GETTING SERIOUS

Introduction

So you're finally ready to rock! Your first gig may well be a bittersweet experience but, if you make it through, there's no experience quite like it. It's what happens next that's important, though – getting more gigs, upping your performance level and growing your audience. Take these seriously, while never forgetting to enjoy yourself, and you could be on your way to superstardom ... well, in a month or two! Even the best bands take time to develop, and it's this part of your journey that can be even more rewarding that what came before.

1

2

3

4

5

6

7

8

9

10

11

12

Developing Your Sound

So what kind of band do you want to be? Your musical style can be defined from the outset – for example, 'we want to sound like Muse' – or can develop from the different inclinations of the musicians involved. In other words, your band may be a motor boat which powers ahead in one direction, or a yacht whose ultimate course is the result of three, four or more different winds blowing on its sail.

It's fair to say the latter approach has been the one taken by many of our most innovative groups. But 'sounding like Muse' (or whoever) will do no harm as a starting point to get you focused. Besides, *you* may think you sound like Muse, but the outside ear

▶ *Matthew Bellamy from Muse. Do you want your band to sound like Muse? The musical styles of bands you like can be a good starting point for developing your own sound.*

could pick up something different. And, even in the sailboat analogy, someone has to take the rudder and make course corrections. This is assuming you are

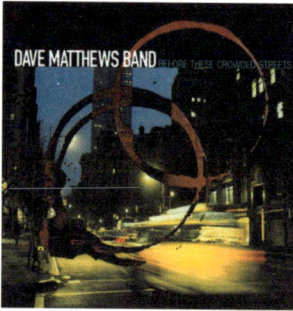

▼ *Dave Matthews of the Dave Matthews Band is the singer, songwriter and guitarist.*

a democracy: if you're the Fred Bloggs Band, and Fred is writing and singing the songs, then the others are unlikely to enjoy as much of a say.

Talking of this, who is going to provide the material – will the songs be covers or originals, group or individual efforts? Lyrics are a good starting point; you won't get too far without them. If someone brings in some words, or at the least some song titles, you can work from there.

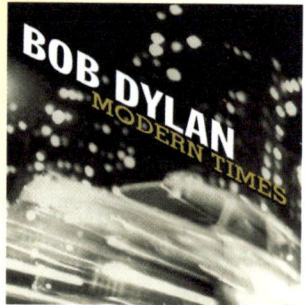

▶ *Bob Dylan is renowned for his lyrics.*

42

▼ *Consider adding new sounds to your music. British band the Guillemots used a typewriter as an 'instrument' in their song 'Who Left The Lights Off, Baby?'*

Consider adding new instruments to broaden your sound, but bear in mind most successful bands have five people or less. Maybe the current members could use their talents to make other sounds? If it doesn't work, move on – but don't get bogged down, keep the momentum going at all costs.

The First Live Performance

Your first time onstage together can be a nerve-wracking experience – it's often painful at the time and almost always something you're glad to have under your belt, especially if you're a 'live virgin'. Expecting people to come and see you do an hour's worth of music first time out is also unrealistic, so a Battle of the Bands or an Open Mic (jam) night would be a good way to lose your virginity. Failing that, find another two bands who are just starting and promote your own show of three short sets at

Talented?
2C0 Student Programming Board Presents
Open Mic Night

Thursday, March 27, 2008 @2C Coffee Bar (2nd floor) 8-10pm

◄ *Open mic nights are a great way to gain experience of performing in front of a live audience.*

a local village hall or club. You'll get three times the audience and may make some useful musician contacts for the future.

Choose songs the audience are likely to know and enjoy, and ones that fit together well. Be prepared for negative as well as positive reaction – it's not the end

▲ *Choose songs the audience are going to enjoy – you are there to entertain them!*

of the world (or the band) if you don't get rave reviews first time out, that's something to aim for in the future. And don't play everything you know – pick the best and leave them wanting more!

Make sure you have a roadie who can pick up knocked-over mic stands. Have at least one spare guitar, tuned before the performance, standing by in case of string breaks, and a fresh set of strings for the roadie to make the necessary running repairs. He/she should also have spare batteries for effects pedals, a spare microphone (if you can afford one), drumsticks and a snare drum skin – drummers can manage without most things, but sticks and a snare are the absolute minimum!

HANDY HINTS

Never prepare for a gig without making sure you have a roll of Gaffa tape to hand. It fixes very nearly anything and everything, and is invaluable for keeping leads, etc., together.

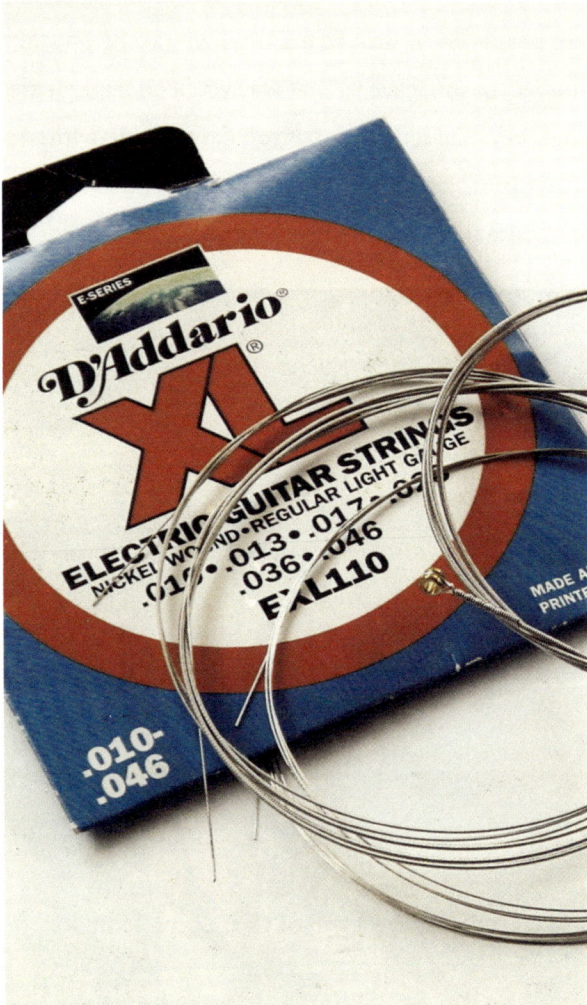

▲ *Bring a spare set of strings to every performance so that you are prepared should any of them break.*

1
2
3
4
5
6
7
8
9
10
11
12

Let people know your name when you come on stage, and when you leave it. That way you'll be remembered and they may come again if you did enough to impress them. Don't look at your shoes – choose a member of the audience to play to, smile and off you go!

▲ *Let people know your name when on stage.*

48

Getting Ready For A Gig

So you've got the songs, you've got the attitude and you want to get out there and show it.

The first thing you need is a set list. This should be agreed before the night and printed out for distribution to everyone – including the sound engineer, if you have one. It is a good idea to have the key of the song in brackets after the title to ensure everyone's in tune, while singers have been known to print their own with the first line of the song under the title to avoid any temporary amnesia. When you've sung the first line, the rest tends to come naturally!

▶ *Makes sure that everyone, including the sound engineer, has a copy of the set list.*

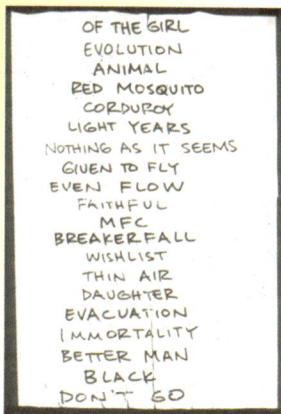

OF THE GIRL
EVOLUTION
ANIMAL
RED MOSQUITO
CORDUROY
LIGHT YEARS
NOTHING AS IT SEEMS
GIVEN TO FLY
EVEN FLOW
FAITHFUL
MFC
BREAKERFALL
WISHLIST
THIN AIR
DAUGHTER
EVACUATION
IMMORTALITY
BETTER MAN
BLACK
DON'T GO

1
2
3
4
5
6
7
8
9
10
11
12

Don't go on stage 'cold' – warm up both your fingers and your voices in the dressing room. A set of scales or exercises always helps: if in doubt sing the octave ('doh-ray-me') and back down again. If you don't have a dressing room, find somewhere suitably out of the way to chill out. Give everybody their space, and help anyone who suffers from stage fright by gently encouraging them.

▼ A checklist of all your equipment may be helpful to ensure that you have everything you need, particularly if you do not have a road manager.

By now everyone should have arrived at the pre-arranged time and brought everything they need. If you don't have a road manager, make sure someone has a checklist of the equipment required so you know you are ready and able to do the gig as well as willing.

◄ Warm up before a performance by playing or singing scales.

HANDY HINTS

Make sure you are at venues with plenty of time to set up and prepare. Threaten frequent non-compliers with a fate worse than death....

Do not indulge in alcohol or other substances before you go on – there's enough to think about, and plenty of time afterwards to reward yourself. Keep a clear head and focus on what you are about to do.

▲ *It is best to celebrate with a drink after the gig and not before.*

Soundchecking

The first time you will pick up your instruments and play is before the audience arrive. This is the soundcheck, the final chance to make sure everything is balanced correctly and one instrument doesn't drown out another.

Choose a number for your soundcheck that includes every element you are likely to use in your performance. This includes backing vocals from every member who contributes them: a 'one, two' into a microphone doesn't count!

. . . .

▲ *Adjust your volume so that everything is balanced correctly and you don't drown another instrument out!*

◄ *A quick 'one, two' into a microphone does not constitute a soundcheck!*

There are two elements of the soundcheck, and both are important. The first is 'front of house' sound, which is what the audience are about to receive. The second is the sound you will hear as a musician onstage. If you have monitors, and you should, can you hear everything you need to from them when playing at performance volume? Also, if you rely on visual cues like the drummer raising his sticks to end a song, can everyone see who they need to?

▲ *If you rely on visual cues, make sure that you can see the person who will be giving them.*

Sometimes soundchecks are not possible. In these cases it's crucial to have someone who can stand at the back of the venue and, by means of hand signals, get band members to tweak their volumes. They, of course, must keep their eyes on this person and put their suggestions into action.

Something else to bear in mind is that a venue may have different sonic characteristics when it's full and empty. Again, having someone in the room as your eyes and ears can help you counteract this before the evening gets too old.

▲ *A venue will have different acoustics when empty and when full, so be prepared to make adjustments.*

Choosing Venues

You're ready to rock the world – now all you need is somewhere to play. Don't expect Wembley first time off; even supergroups had to start somewhere.

And many of those big-name bands have found themselves going down like lead balloons when, at the start of their careers, they were booked into inappropriate venues. But what exactly is appropriate?

The first thing to do is pay a visit on a gig night and see who is playing and how they're going down. Take a

▲*You may not be able to fill a venue like Wembley Stadium yet, but you've got to start somewhere.*

◄ For over 30 years the CBGB club in Manhattan was the world's most famous punk-rock club. Choose a venue that suits your type of music.

flyer or make a note of forthcoming acts and do a little Internet research to find out what music they play.

Is there a dress code at the venue, and if so will your audience comply? Is there an age limit, and are your potential fans old enough to get in (this particularly applies to licensed premises)?

► Does the venue have a dress code? If so, will your audience comply?

Approaching Venues

If all feels good, approach the venue with a CD of yourselves, plus a 'press release' (written description of who you are with contact details) and a photo. Follow this up in a week (before they forget about you), making sure you've got the name and number of the man/woman with the say-so. When you make your follow-up call, give them positive news (radio play, media coverage, other gigs, new band mates, etc.). Delivered politely, this will give you a chance to impress them and get the gig you want.

◄ Present a venue that you would like to play at with a CD of your music and a press release. Don't forget to chase them up with a phone call a week later.

▼ *Playing at local summer festivals could expose you and your music to a whole new audience.*

You probably won't earn much on your first appearance but once you've pulled a crowd and gone down well you will be in a good position to up your fee. Make sure to agree what you're going to get in advance and in writing if possible: email the venue with confirmation of how long you're playing and the payment that has been agreed – you then have this to fall back on.

Finally, think outside the box. Does your town have a summer festival, or does a local charity need a fundraiser? You may not get paid much but the audience – and the spinoffs – could be massive. So go for it!

Getting Gigs

The first gigs you play will undoubtedly have been found by yourselves. Only when you have a 'buzz' going will any of the professionals be interested in a piece of the action. If you have a natural leader in the band or, even better, an outgoing friend who will act as your manager then that will take a lot of the hassle out of things: making it a combined responsibility seldom brings the desired results.

Another possibility is approaching a band you admire and/or have a musical affinity with. Ask them if they would consider you for a support slot when next in your area. Playing half an hour of music to a supportive crowd would do your confidence a power of good, it would be something to put on your CV and, if you can get local club owners or promoters to attend, could give you a real leg-up in status.

● ●

▶ *The first gigs you play will undoubtedly have been found by yourselves.*

HANDY HINTS

Always supply the venue you're playing with posters at least a week beforehand. That way you'll get a buzz going.

◄ On their first tour
of the US Led Zeppelin
supported the band Iron
Butterfly. However, the
audience enjoyed Led
Zeppelin's performance
so much that Iron
Butterfly refused
to follow them.

Becoming part of a booking agent's 'stable' is attractive, but you have to prove that you have audience-pulling potential first. The agent will take a percentage of your earnings, but if they up your fee then you may be no worse off and, depending how often you work, possibly even better off.

HANDY HINTS

Take any support gig offered. Even if the money's no good you may make useful contacts and impress the venue enough to get your own gig.

It's important to be with a supportive agent, and one with contacts in the areas that are useful for you. If you don't want to play further than five miles from home, or you are a punk band and they specialize in booking functions or weddings, your 'marriage' is likely to be short and not very sweet.

▼ *An agent with contacts in areas that are useful to you will help you get gigs.*

◄ *You will have to be able to prove your audience-pulling potential before you will be able to find an agent.*

Improving Stage Presence

The biggest challenge when moving from rehearsal room to the live stage is projection. It's no longer enough to play, you have to entertain. And to do that you have to project your personality from the stage to the room.

A good strategy is to pick someone at the back of the room and play to them. If you are projecting yourself that far, then you will be doing all right for the rest of the audience. Keep your head up, look happy to be there (if you don't why should they?) and do your level best to entertain.

If you are an originals band, give the audience a few insights into what they are about to hear (who wrote it, what it's about). If you are selling CDs then let them

▶ *Madonna performing; when you get on stage it's no longer enough to play or sing, you have to entertain.*

know which songs they can hear again. If you're a covers band, or include covers with originals, space the famous ones out through the set to give the audience some recognition points.

Hopefully you have a number or two that you can encourage the audience to join in with. Don't try this in the first few songs; they won't have warmed up yet.

HANDY HINTS

Think about investing in stage lighting. It's not always necessary but it's cheaper than you think and adds a professional touch to your show.

◄ *Jay Z working the room. Few bands succeed as static attractions.*

If your singer has a radio microphone or a mic with a long lead he/she can get down off the stage and 'work the room', which is often an effective tactic. The singer, at least, should make a point of moving around – few bands succeed as static attractions. And have a think about your stage wardrobe – what signal is it sending?

The best way to develop your stage presence and act is to have a friend film your performance. Then go through it with them, encouraging them to point out the good and the bad (if you can't see it yourself). It's a never-ending process, but well worth it if you want to grow as performers.

▲ *Getting a friend to video you can help you assess your performance and improve your weaknesses.*

Gaining A Following

It's amazing how many bands you see who get on stage without telling the audience who they are. There are three main opportunities – when you come on, when you leave the stage and making individual introductions in the middle.

Having told them who you are, why not invite potential fans to join your mailing list – leave a clipboard, paper and pen prominently by the stage – or duplicate some flyers telling them where and when you are playing next. And don't forget to direct them to your website.

HANDY HINTS

Always keep your website/MySpace page up to date with the latest gigs – otherwise you'll look lame.

▼ *Leave a clipboard and pen by the stage for people to leave their contact details so that you can add them to your mailing list.*

Business cards printed up with the band name, logo and your contact details will always come in handy to pass to people who show interest. If the CDs you are using to get gigs are good, print some labels and offer them to your fans at a reasonable price. Best not to put more than four songs per disc, or they may stay at home and enjoy the set from their armchair!

HANDY HINTS

Tell your fans to let venues know how much they enjoyed the show and how they'll be coming back for the next one – it'll help make sure there is one!

◄ *Sending an email newsletter to your fans, letting them know what you're up to and when and where you will be playing, is a great way of creating interest.*

Before the next month's worth of gigs, send out an email newsletter to your fans letting them know where and when you are playing. Mention any new songs, band members or things you're going to add to your act to pique their curiosity.

HANDY HINTS

Develop a relationship with your local paper/radio station and get your gigs listed. Invite their showbiz reporter to come and see you – they might do a feature!

If the venues you are playing have a website make sure they are advertising your show and see if they will post a web link to your site.

▼ *Make sure that the venue you are playing at is advertising your gig on its website.*

Finally, get some cheap t-shirts and design some iron-on logos you can put on the chest and sell at cost or a little more. You're not only getting into the world

of merchandising but also letting your fans show their allegiance!

▶ *Get some plain t-shirts and print your logo on them for fans to buy.*

Summary

Check your progress against this list

Find ways of getting live experience
at jam nights, etc.................................. ☐

Enter Battle of the Bands competitions
to measure yourselves against others .... ☐

Find suitable venues to play and
approach them politely but persistently .... ☐

Offer your services free for charity fundraisers, etc.. ☐

Work on your stage presence; video
yourselves and study the results................. ☐

Get a stage wardrobe together that
works for the band as a whole.................... ☐

Let people know who you are when
you are on stage .... ☐

Use t-shirts, posters etc. to promote
your name and logo .... ☐

Start a mailing list for your fans and email them
every month with news and upcoming gigs....... ☐

Get merchandising!.............................. ☐

HOME RECORDING

Not so long ago, the only way to get a master-quality recording was to use a state of the art pro studio, but all that has changed. These days, putting together a home studio is both an achievable and affordable option, and in this chapter we'll be looking at what you need to do to get started. Don't be diverted by the jargon – read, learn and record!

SETTING UP A HOME STUDIO

3

Introduction

Setting up your own recording studio is nowhere near as difficult as it once was, but there are a number of things you'll need to think about carefully. In this section, you'll find advice on preparing the room itself, and on making sure you've got the basic equipment you'll need before you can start recording. We'll look at the recording and mixing process and offer some ideas for putting together that all-important debut album, or a killer demo. We'll also explore the world of file formats, file-sharing and downloads, all essential if you want to get your music out to the widest possible audience.

The Home Recording Studio

Whatever style of music you play, the studio is where everything comes together, and all those hours spent writing and rehearsing are turned into something that shows the world just what you can do. You can think of the studio itself as another instrument – the more you practise and experiment, the more you'll learn about getting the best out of your set-up.

The simplest home studios are based around a computer, using an audio interface and soundcard to capture the basic tracks, and sequencing software to perform the mixing and mastering. If you intend to work alone, and if you like to experiment with sounds and textures, this sort of set-up has a lot to offer – but most artists will want to add much more to the mix, including vocals and real instruments. Stand-alone digital

► *A computer, with the appropriate soundcard, sequencer software, virtual instruments and plug-in effects, is essential.*

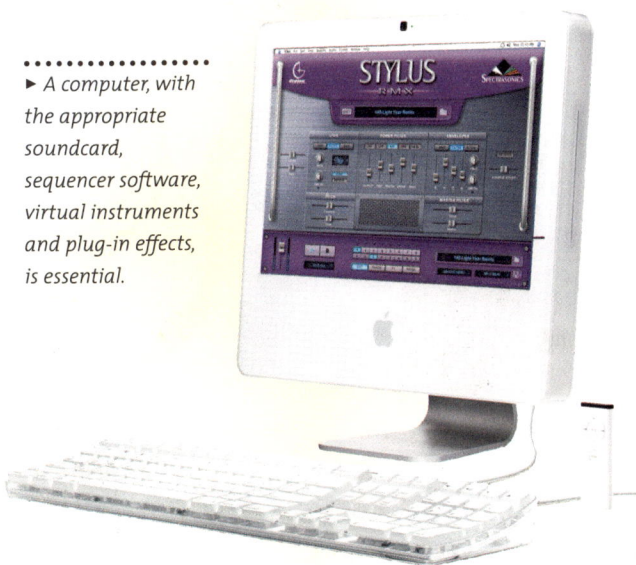

◄ *Practice and experimentation in the home recording studio will pay off.*

▼ *You will probably want to add real instruments to the mix.*

multitrack recorders, which have similar processing and mixing capabilities to computer-based software, offer far greater flexibility in these circumstances. Many recent examples can be linked to a computer via USB or FireWire connections to allow even more options.

The gear you eventually choose will depend on the sort of music you're aiming to record, the space you have available to do it in and how much money you have to spend. There's a huge range of hardware and software available to help you record, edit, mix and master your music prior to unleashing it on the world, and these days it's possible to produce professional-sounding results on a bargain-basement budget.

▲ *You can produce a professional-sounding recording on a bargain-basement budget.*

The Basic Tools Required

When you're setting your studio up, think about how much space you're going to need, not just for the gear itself, but also to accommodate additional instruments and the people who'll be playing them. Make sure you do everything you can to create what the professionals call a 'neutral' room – one that minimizes reflected sound, and allows you to capture that all-important vocal or acoustic guitar overdub as faithfully as possible. If you have a hard floor, put down rugs or carpeting. Sound reflected from walls can be more difficult to deal with, but hanging up sheets or curtaining should do the trick.

HANDY HINTS

Allow yourself more room than you need, especially if you plan to have 'non-virtual' musicians contributing to your recordings. They will need space for amplifiers, etc.

Getting The Gear

A good home studio with quality gear is always preferable to a bigger set-up with cheaper gear – don't forget, the better the end-product, the more attention you're likely to attract, so always go for the best gear you can afford. Make sure you've got decent microphones and enough stands to attach them to, and don't forget that each microphone will need its own pre-amp to boost the signal to a usable line level.

▲ *Always buy the best equipment you can afford. You can't go wrong with a versatile dynamic microphone like the Shure SM57.*

HANDY HINTS

If you're using separate pre-amps for your microphones, get the best quality you can afford. The better the source, the better the final result.

Monitor speakers aren't essential, but they are much better than headphones for playback during the mixing and mastering processes. Of course, if you need to keep the noise down, headphones will be your only option.

▲ *Monitor speakers are better than headphones for playback.*

One of the most important decisions you need to make is what you're going to record your music to – although computers are at the heart of many home studios, some people prefer to record and mix on a stand-alone multitrack recorder, and we'll look at the possibilities offered by each option in the next section. Whichever route you follow, ensure you have enough channels and inputs for all the gear you're likely to want to connect up.

▲ *Some people prefer to record and mix on multitrack recorders.*

▼ *If you're building your studio around a computer, you'll need some sequencing software.*

Finally, if you're building your studio around a computer, you'll need some sequencing software. As you move forward, you'll probably add sample libraries and softsynths to your arsenal, but for now this should give you everything you need to get started.

HANDY HINTS

Look at flat-pack furniture stores like Ikea for a suitable computer desk – they have a variety of off-the-shelf solutions to keeping everything neat and tidy.

Laying Down Tracks

There are no hard-and-fast rules when it comes to recording your music – so much depends on the type of music you're making, the instruments you're using and the facilities available.

Traditionally, recordings are done in layers, each instrument or group of instruments being added to those already recorded. It's normal to record the drums

▲ *Drums are normally recorded first, providing a solid foundation to build everything else on.*

1
2
3
4
5
6
7
8
9
10
11
12

HANDY HINTS

Make sure your chosen location has no noise issues – either sounds intruding into your studio or sound escaping from it to the neighbours' annoyance!

first – after all, everyone else needs to know how fast to play, so it's a logical place to start. Whether you're using a drum emulator, or playing live against a click track, the percussion provides a solid foundation to build everything else on. Bass is usually the next item on the agenda, completing a musical foundation on top of which your other instruments can be added as required. Vocals should be recorded last, to make sure they are clearly audible above the music, with any backing vocals being added once the lead is in place.

► *Vocals should be recorded last, to make sure they are clearly audible above the music.*

Overdubbing

This process, known as overdubbing, allows you to go back and re-record as many times as you want to achieve the best possible result. Each overdub gets its own channel, so it's easy to replace any individual voice or instrument at a later stage. It's an extremely flexible process – you could, for example, record a synthesized bass-line as a guide, then replace it with a feed from a real bass guitar at a later session.

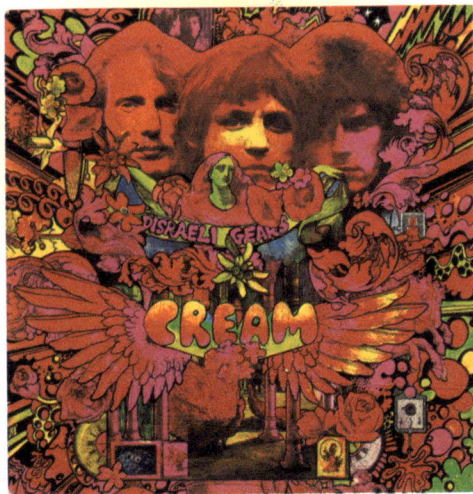

▲ *Overdubbing enabled Eric Clapton to play both rhythm and lead guitar on 'Sunshine of Your Love' on Cream's* Disraeli Gears *(1967).*

1
2
3
4
5
6
7
8
9
10
11
12

It's probably better to add effects after you've recorded the individual instruments – recording 'dry' encourages you to concentrate on playing a better take, and you can always add effects at a later stage. Try things out, find the methods that work for you – there are no rights and wrongs, but following a few basic guidelines may make the whole process a lot smoother.

▲ *Concentrate on playing well when recording and add effects later.*

Putting Together An Album

Everyone has their own opinion about what makes a good album, but you can give yourself a much better chance of success if you follow a few basic principles.

The most important thing is consistency – you need good, solid songs, and everyone has to be able to stand alone as well as sounding good in the context of the album. Before you include any track, ask yourself whether it really represents you and what you want to say, and whether it's likely to make people want to hear more of your music.

▲ *What do you think makes a great album?*

91

HANDY HINTS

When you're recording, create a timetable to give yourself a goal. Eighty per cent of the work takes half the time, so don't obsess too much on the final refinements – it's probably nearly there!

When people listen to your album, you want them to stay with it from beginning to end. Being consistent doesn't mean that every track has to sound like every other track, and the best albums have a mixture of fast, medium and slow songs, but making sure that there's a natural progression from one song to the next is crucial.

OK COMPUTER
RADIOHEAD

◄ *The lyrics of Radiohead's album* OK Computer *(1997) consistently emphasize common themes such as consumerism, social disconnection, political stagnation and modern malaise.*

Song Selection

Don't be tempted to put too much on the album. Even if you think you've got 14 or 15 sure-fire winners, the chances are that some of them are better than others, so try to include only your very best efforts. The more tracks you include, the greater the chance that people will skip some of them, but keep it short and sweet and you'll reduce that risk. Make sure the opening number grabs their attention and draws them in, and the last one leaves them hungry for more.

Similar principles apply to demo recordings. When producing a demo CD, make sure you put your best songs first, and keep it brief – four or five tracks at the most, because that's all anyone you send it to will listen to.

▲ *Only put your very best work on your demo CD – be selective.*

Burning The Album To CD

3

Burning your music to CD is one of the simplest parts of the process, although as always, there are some points to consider.

Before you start, you'll need to make sure that the music you've recorded has been saved in a format that your CD-burning software can handle. Most sequencing software will enable you to save your work

▲ *Burning your music to CD is relatively simple, but make sure that you record it in either a WAV or AIFF format.*

in a variety of formats, and to ensure you get full CD quality reproduction, you need to save either to WAV format if you're using a Windows-based computer, or AIFF format if you're using a Mac. Make sure that the save settings are the same as the record settings – 44.1 kHz, 16-bit, stereo.

Many of the Digital Audio Workstation packages include file-conversion and CD-burning software, but if you're using one that doesn't, you'll need to make sure that you have separate software to do the job. Whether you use Windows or a Mac, there are a number of commercially available CD-burning programmes, including those by Roxio and Nero, as well as a wide range of free downloads, including SimplyBurns, LiquidCD, Burn, Burn My Files, CDBurnXP and Express Burn.

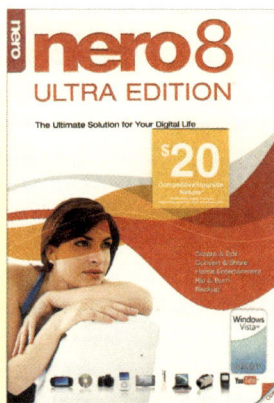

▲ *Nero is a commercially available CD-burning programme.*

◄ *LiquidCD and Burn are just two CD-burning programmes that you can download free from the Internet.*

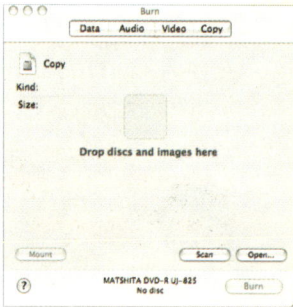

Most of the CD-burning programmes will be able to convert and burn WAV and AIFF files to CD. In addition, you'll often be able to add data that will display the track titles when the CD is playing. You'll also be able to choose how the tracks are sequenced, whether or not there are short gaps between them and how fast to burn the disc – a slower speed may be better to ensure the best quality reproduction.

Once you've burned your disc, play it back on a CD player and on your computer, to make sure it plays and sounds the way you want it to.

▼ *You can download CDBurnXP from http://cdburnerxp.se*

HANDY HINTS

Invite outside criticism; send MP3s or demo CDs to people whose opinion you trust and take note of their feedback.

Summary

Check your progress against this list

Think about how much space
you're going to need . . . . ☐

Always go for the best gear you can afford . . . . . . ☐

Make sure you've got decent microphones . . . . . . ☐

Record the drums first then add effects after
you've recorded the individual instruments . . . . . ☐

Don't be tempted to put too much
on the album . . . . ☐

Put your best songs first, and keep it brief . . . . . . ☐

Ensure that the music has been saved in a
format your CD-burning software can handle . . . ☐

CHOOSING THE RIGHT EQUIPMENT

4

Introduction

Even if you are well up on all the acronyms, product names and formats available, choosing the right equipment for a home studio can be a confusing and daunting prospect. The best solution is to get advice from people who have picked their way through the minefield and lived to tell the tale. Meanwhile, read up as much as you can on the subject so you can make best use of the advice given.

Choosing The Right Hardware

The main limitation when buying equipment for your studio is the available budget. But if your shopping list consists of only what you really need, you may be pleasantly surprised. The cost of recording gear is considerably less than it was just a few years ago, and if you shop around you can pick up some amazing bargains, especially on Internet auction sites. But you need to know what you're doing, especially in terms of achieving a set-up with potential to expand at the same rate as your abilities and budget.

◄ *When choosing equipment your main limitation is likely to be your budget.*

Modern studio gear offers numerous ways of achieving the same end result, and talking to people who know about the options and how everything fits together is paramount. One of the prime sources of confusion is that there are so many pieces of equipment that combine the functions of two, three or even more bits of traditional kit, so talking about a 'mixer' or an 'audio interface' (and whether you'll even need one) can be confusing in itself.

▲ *The Yamaha N12 Digital Mixing Studio is a mixing console and an audio interface in one.*

HANDY HINTS

In general, keep it as simple as possible when buying studio equipment – buy the gear you really need before the gear you might like to have, and make sure you get the best you can afford.

The Apple Macintosh has been the computer format of choice for professional sound recording for many years – although the PC is, of course, a very valid alternative – and now comes with GarageBand software pre-installed. If nothing else, this gives hands-on experience of recording music on a computer and is a handy and cost-effective way of 'learning the ropes'. There may be a distance between the capabilities of GarageBand and the Pro Tools professional-standard used by the big bands, but just as airline pilots first learned to fly on small training planes, the principles are very much common to both.

▼ *The Apple Macintosh has been the computer format of choice for professional sound recording technicians for many years.*

4

Music

HANDY HINTS

Today there's very little to choose between PCs and Macs when it comes to setting up a home studio – each will provide a good basis for your set-up, so go with whatever you're used to.

Computer

Unless you're planning to use a stand-alone multitrack digital recorder, the computer is the heart of the home recording studio, so it's essential to make sure your computer is up to the job.

With digital audio, speed and performance are paramount – make sure you get the fastest processor, the biggest hard-drive and as much memory as you can afford. Simply recording digital audio involves huge amounts of data, and you'll be handling even more as soon as you start editing and mixing your music.

▲ *The computer is the heart of the home recording studio.*

HANDY HINTS

Don't let a computer hard drive failure destroy all your hard work – after every session, back-up your recordings to an external hard drive and disconnect it from the computer once they're safely transferred.

There are new analogue mixer/audio interface devices on the market that allow you to record and process your music without a soundcard, since they connect to the computer via a FireWire port, but these tend to be very expensive. If you intend to use a more traditional set-up, make sure you have a good soundcard – a PCI interface is best. Avoid USB unless you intend to record no more than one or two tracks at a time, since USB simply isn't up to the job of handling the data volumes involved.

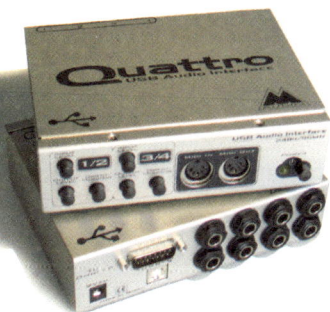

◄ This M-Audio Quattro is a high-quality USB audio interface. However, FireWire interfaces are generally better.

Take some time out to look at the options – remember that most off-the-shelf computers are not put together with music production in mind, and building a machine that's designed for the purpose may well be a better way to go. It's an important part of the set-up, so make sure you think it through.

▲ *Most computers are not built with music production in mind, so consider buying a purpose-built machine.*

HANDY HINTS

If your budget will stretch to it, there are benefits to purpose-built audio computers, including hardware and software compatibility, tailor-made components and dedicated customer support.

Audio Interface

The next thing to think about is how you're going to connect instruments and microphones to the computer. There are various ways you can achieve this, but the cheapest and most straightforward is to use an audio interface.

Again, you'll need to choose carefully, taking into account what sort of music you're going to be producing, and how many inputs you're likely to need at any time. As a minimum, your audio interface should have two microphone pre-amp inputs, which would allow you to record two vocalists, or a vocalist and acoustic guitar.

HANDY HINTS

When buying your gear, try to work out your immediate needs, and then think about how things might develop over the next few years. Get this right, and you'll be able to enjoy the benefits of a settled working environment.

If you've got plenty of space, and you intend to record drums, you'll need at least four microphone inputs – one for the bass drum, one for the snare and two overheads.

In general, go for as many inputs as you can afford – it gives room for expansion, and takes care of anything you've overlooked. Check the retailer's return policy – you can usually try stuff and return it if you find it's not right for you.

Think about how you're going to link the audio interface to your computer – it's almost certainly worth going the extra mile and investing in an audio interface with a FireWire connection to give you more flexibility as your music develops.

▲ *The Edirol FA101 FireWire audio interface can handle 10 channels of input/output.*

▼ *It's worth investing in an audio interface with a FireWire connection.*

HANDY HINTS

With today's hi-tech studio solutions, you'll often find pieces of equipment that will perform more than one function; before you spend your hard-earned cash, do as much research as you can – talk to the experts, check out online forums and don't be afraid to ask questions.

Software Sequencers

Some audio interfaces come with bundled sequencing software – Yamaha gear comes with Cubase, and M-Audio with Pro Tools – so look at what's on offer before you buy sequencing software for your PC. If your audio interface doesn't include software, double check to make sure it's going to be compatible with the software you intend to use.

If you're using a Mac, the GarageBand software that you'll find pre-installed on most new machines, coupled with a soundcard adapter for instruments,

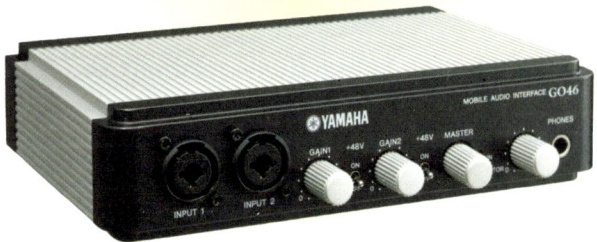

▲ *The Yamaha GO46 audio interface comes with Cubase sequencing software.*

▼ *GarageBand software allows you to record without an audio interface.*

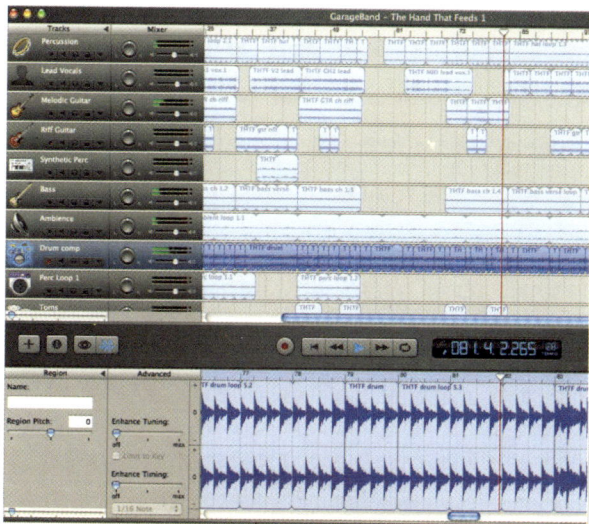

will allow you to record without an audio interface, and there are now USB microphones available that make things even easier. Using GarageBand is a cost-effective way to go for beginners, but offers only limited audio processing options, so you may want to explore other possibilities as you progress.

MIDI Sequencers

MIDI, which stands for Musical Instrument Digital Interface, is an essential component of every modern studio from the biggest professional set-ups to the one-man home-based operation.

In simple terms, MIDI is software or hardware designed to make and manage computer-generated music. It's an industry standard, so any MIDI-compatible device

▲ *Most people imagine something like these MIDI cables when they hear the word MIDI because they think of it as a way of connecting instruments. MIDI is actually a language used to convey musical performances.*

▼ *The synthesizer started it all. The MIDI revolution began as a result of electronic musical-instrument companies wanting their instruments to communicate with each other.*

can communicate with any other MIDI-compatible device. It's important to understand that MIDI files do not contain audio data – they're simply a way of storing the information required to trigger a specific, predictable response from an instrument voice bank or a software sample library.

MIDI-compatible devices are generally referred to as MIDI controllers, and most often take the form of a piano-style keyboard, although there are many other types, including drum pads and guitar controllers. Even saxes, clarinets and other wind instruments can be reproduced by using an EWI (Electronic Wind Instrument), which features a pressure-sensitive mouthpiece and keys to control the eventual sound.

▼ *Saxes, clarinets and other wind instruments can be reproduced using an EWI such as this Akai EWI USB wind instrument controller.*

Many sequencers will work with MIDI data alongside audio data, although you need to check carefully when you're selecting your computer software to make sure it does what you'll want it to do. Sonar, Cubase, Pro Tools, Ableton and Logic are all equally at home with audio and MIDI files, but if you're on a budget, or thinking about freeware, you'll need to do some research. To confuse matters even more, some sequencers will work with software MIDI (softsynths), but not hardware MIDI (voice banks or external instruments), so be on your guard.

► *Pro Tools is equally at home with audio and MIDI files, but some freeware may not be.*

Synthesizers

Early synthesizers were dedicated hardware instruments, normally controlled via a piano-style keyboard, which offered musicians access to an ever-wider range of electronic sounds as the technology developed. Before long, synthesizers were capable of fairly accurate imitations of other instruments, and it is in this area that their modern counterpart, the softsynths or virtual instruments, excel.

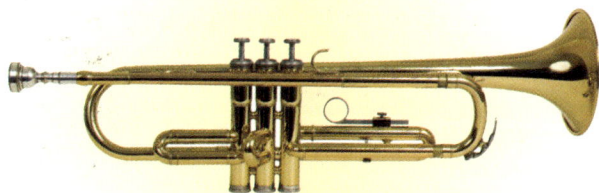

Dedicated hardware synthesizers haven't gone away – many players still use them in live performance, largely because they have a physical interface (knobs and sliders) that make them easier to control on stage. In the studio, however, softsynths have grown in

▲ *Synthesizers imitate the sound of other instruments.*

117

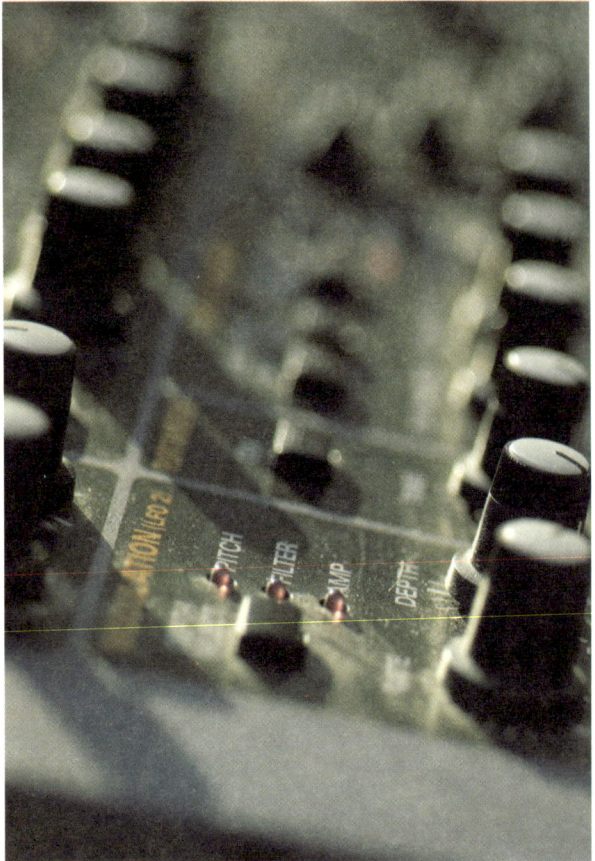

popularity – they're cheaper than the hardware versions, far more portable, and they interface very easily with your sequencing software. Not only that, but they offer almost limitless possibilities for musicians of any age or experience, working in any style.

◄ *Hardware synthesizers have not gone away – many players still use them in live performance.*

Softsynths make it simple to add whatever you need to your recordings – it could be a string or brass section, the sound of a particular drum kit or simply an instrument that no one in the band can play. Many softsynths emulate the circuitry and components of hardware synthesizers, including the early analogue instruments that still find favour among enthusiasts today. Not only do they produce the same sounds,

▲ *Synthesizers make it easy to add a string or brass section to your recordings.*

▼ *Many synthesizers, such as this software model, offer an abundant library of easily located and used sounds. This can speed up production and let you focus on composition.*

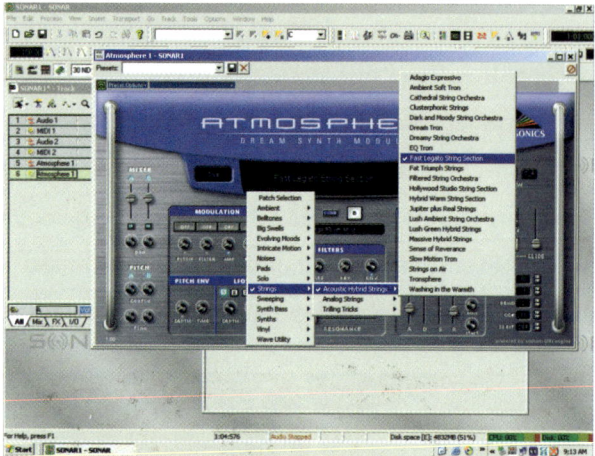

many of these emulators even offer on-screen graphical representations of the controls found on the original instruments.

Other softsynths are mostly sample-based, and there are lots of free online sample libraries that allow you to add even more sounds to your repertoire. Compatibility is not usually a problem, but always check that the softsynth you're thinking of getting is compatible with the sequencing software you're already using.

Mixers

By using an audio interface and computer-based sequencer software, you can get by without using a hardware mixer, and this set-up would probably suit those on a tight budget. Simply use a multi-input audio interface, connect it to the computer and do your mixing on the sequencer. If you prefer a more traditional mixing desk, with knobs and faders, you could then add a Control Surface to let you adjust the levels and effects in the software mixer.

▲ *If you would prefer to use a traditional mixing desk, try adding the Mackie Universal Pro: a Control Surface that lets you adjust the levels and effects in the software mixer.*

▼ *If you do decide to invest in a mixer, make sure that it has lots of simultaneous inputs.*

A hardware mixer, also referred to as a mixing board or mixing console, offers greater flexibility, especially if you're planning to use a lot of real instruments in your work. If you intend to record a whole band, you'll need a mixer that can handle lots of simultaneous inputs – don't forget, drums alone would require at least four microphone pre-amp connections, and then there are hardware synths and guitars to consider. If you're

HANDY HINTS

The knobs and faders on mixing desks and Control Surfaces need to be well-made to stand up to repeated use. If you're buying one, be prepared to pay a little more to ensure quality – this is one item where you'll get what you pay for.

using outboard effects units – reverbs, delays, guitar pedals and so on – you'll find a mixer by far the best way to link everything up to the recording gear.

There are two types of mixer – analogue and digital – and each has its own advantages. Which will be better for you will depend on the gear you're planning to link up, and the way you intend to record, so take some time out to research your options before you buy. One final thought: a mixer is a major investment, but if you decide you need one, make sure you choose one that has enough inputs to take care of your current needs and a few spares to cover future growth.

▲ *The Yamaha L69 is a digital mixer; whether you choose a digital or an analogue mixer will depend on the gear you're planning to link it up to.*

123

Speakers

Loudspeakers designed for use in a recording studio are usually known as studio monitors or reference monitors. Although they don't look any different, they're not the same as the type of loudspeaker you see on hi-fi systems – hi-fi speakers are designed to play commercially produced recordings, which are subject to compression, and the cheaper ones often favour certain frequency ranges in order to produce a more user-friendly overall sound.

Studio monitors have a totally different role – in the studio, you'll often be playing back a raw mix, an uncompressed recording that can have large variations in volume and sudden bursts of

▶ *Monitors may look like regular hi-fi speakers but they are not the same.*

▼ *In a studio you are listening to uncompressed recordings that can have large variations in volume and sudden bursts of sound.*

4

sound quite unlike a commercial recording. Not only that, but speakers that favour certain frequencies are no good when it comes to mastering or mixing your music. You need to be able to hear exactly what's going on, so studio monitors are designed to have as 'flat' a frequency response as possible. When you're listening in the studio, you'll often be in close proximity to the monitors, so they are also built to project the sound in a different way to hi-fi speakers.

Of course, you can always use headphones to listen to your mixes, but a set of studio monitors will give you

HANDY HINTS

When you're choosing monitor speakers for your studio, listen to as many as possible before you buy. Check out local suppliers, take along some CDs of music similar to what you intend to produce, and ask to hear the music through the speakers to see how they perform.

◄ *Studio monitors are designed to have as 'flat' a frequency response as possible.*

the best chance of producing a recording that will sound good in as many situations as possible. They're not cheap – expect to pay upwards of £100 even for the budget models – but they're an important element of any professional-sounding studio set-up.

▶ *Although you can use headphones to listen to your mixes, a set of studio monitors is best.*

Peripherals & Optional Extras

There are a few other important items you'll need to have around when you're recording – things that are easy to overlook when you're busy making big decisions about the studio's main components.

First of all, if you plan to add vocals to your recordings, make sure you've got enough microphone stands and that they're equipped with pop filters. These filters eliminate the popping and hissing noises that occur naturally when we speak or sing and are an essential aid to getting a professional-standard vocal sound. Spare microphone stands are always a good idea, especially if you also regularly record physical instruments, such as guitars, through amplifiers.

▲ *A pop filter eliminates the popping and hissing noises that occur naturally when we speak or sing.*

HANDY HINTS

If you're suffering from electrical interference on your recordings, look into the possibility of using power conditioners, or filters, to remove unwanted noise.

Make sure you've got all the right cables. When you buy your hardware, you'll often find that the cables you need are included, but it's worth checking. It's also worth having some spare examples of the more commonly used cables around – there's nothing more irritating than setting up a session only to find that you don't have a working microphone cable or guitar lead.

HANDY HINTS

Poor-quality cables can make the best equipment in the world sound bad, so make sure there's enough in your budget for some decent cables to put everything together.

▼ *Make sure you've got all the right cables.*

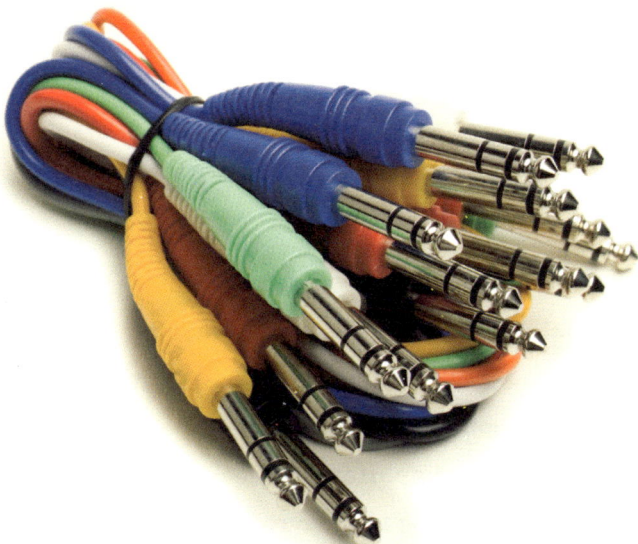

HANDY HINTS

Making your own cables from premium-quality components will always be the most economical and flexible way to connect up all your gear. You can pick up some useful tips on soldering techniques at www.kpsec.freeuk.com and www.leadsdirect.f9.co.uk

Headphones, Storage & Power Outlets

Don't forget to get a good set of headphones that you can use when overdubbing vocals, or adding any instruments you're recording via a microphone. And while on the subject of recording vocals, it's important to make sure that the headphones don't leak sound that can be picked up by the vocal microphone.

Also look at racking and storage. If you're keeping things really simple, you may not need much, but keeping things tidy and to hand will create a much better creative environment, and may prolong the life of your gear.

••

▶ *Keep everything tidy with a bit of storage.*

Finally, check the number of power outlets you need and plan accordingly with appropriate extensions. And make sure your equipment is protected by circuit-breakers – it's a small outlay when compared to the cost of repairing or replacing gear.

Finding The Right Software

Just as the price of recording equipment has gone down in the last few years, so adequate software is within the grasp of many more aspiring musicians/producers. Cheap and even free software can do a more than passable job, while the availability of GarageBand software pre-installed on Mac computers has led to an explosion of interest. Checking out some of the websites listed on the following pages before you purchase could save you a lot of time, money and trouble.

▲ *GarageBand software comes pre-installed Mac computers.*

◄ Unfortunately, not all software will work with other software or on every computer.

Compatibility is the major stumbling block: put simply, everything will not work with everything else. So when it comes to augmenting your set-up with plug-ins, do the necessary research before committing to buy something that may prove incompatible. The trend, though, is towards multi-compatibility, so hopefully this will not be a problem too much longer.

The best advice, as ever, is find someone who's done it before, either personally or via a website or bulletin board. They will probably have made the mistakes you want to avoid and will probably be only too happy to help you avoid the same pitfalls. Ask an audio expert and you're on your way to becoming one yourself.

▲ Get advice from someone who has bought and used audio software before you buy.

Plug-ins

Plug-ins are typically third-party software that add features or functionality to an existing application. There are literally thousands of plug-ins available to expand the capabilities of your studio software, allowing you to introduce hundreds of new sounds and instruments into the mix, or to add a wide range of effects to those you already have.

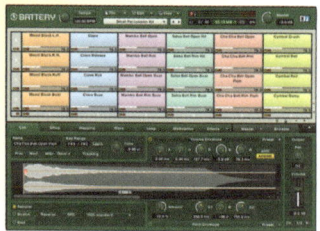

▲ *There are literally thousands of plug-ins available to expand the capabilities of your studio software.*

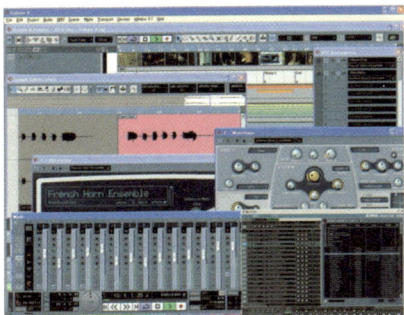

◄ *Make sure that each plug-in is compatible with the software you're already running; for example, Cubase requires VST compatible plug-ins.*

You'll need to make sure that each plug-in is compatible with the software you're already running – there are several different plug-in technologies in use, so check to see which one your software uses. Some of the most popular sequencing applications, including Sonar, Ableton Live and Cubase, require VST (Virtual Studio Technology)-compatible plug-ins, whilst others, such as GarageBand, Logic Express and most Mac OS X-based applications, need AU (Audio Units) compatibility. You'll find that many of the plug-ins currently available have multiple compatibility.

Virtual instrument plug-ins, or softsynths, can provide almost any additional instruments you'll ever need. From vintage analogue synthesizers to complete orchestras, there's no limit to the instrumental possibilities they offer, and there's a wide range of drum synthesizers to choose from as well. Not only that, but there are guitar amp emulators so you can get exactly the sound you need for a particular riff or solo.

These additions to your arsenal needn't break the bank – there are dozens of well-established websites offering a wide range of plug-ins that are free to download, so you've nothing to lose when trying them out.

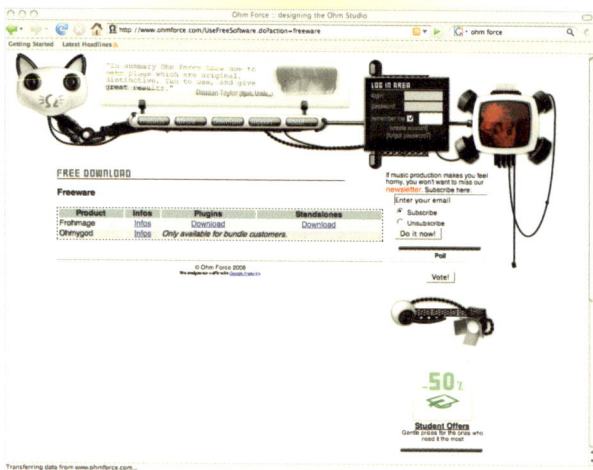

▲ *A wide range of plug-ins are free to download; for example, the Frohmage filter plug-in from www.ohmforce.com*

Editing Software

Editing software is at the heart of the Digital Audio Workstation, and typically allows you to record a number of inputs, store the recordings as digital audio, and then edit and manipulate them using a variety of effects and other functions. Tracks can be faded in and out, made louder or quieter or panned across the stereo image. Sections of music can be moved around, copied and pasted, or simply removed, giving you almost limitless options when it comes to deciding how the finished recording will sound.

4

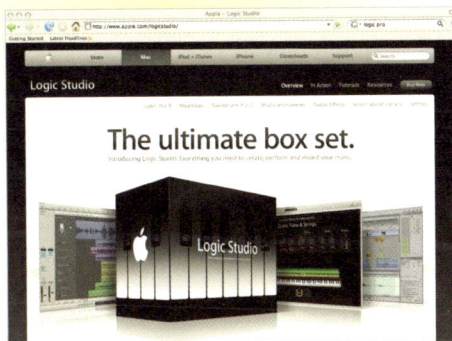

▶ Editing software, such as Apple's Logic, is at the heart of the Digital Audio Workstation.

◄ *You can edit and manipulate recordings in programmes such as Pro Tools.*

Most, but not all, editing software will allow you to import and process MIDI data alongside the digital audio, allowing you to bring the softsynths that were covered in the previous section into the mix.

You'll be able to change the smallest detail, right down to the length of individual notes, or the exact point at which a drum beat falls, and once everything is exactly where you want it, you'll be able to apply a range of effects to improve the overall sound. What's more, if you're unhappy with the changes you've made, you'll have

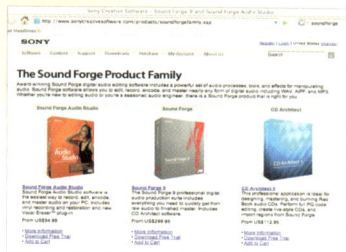

▲ *Find out more about Sony's Sound Forge editing software at www.sonycreativesoftware.com/products/soundforgefamily.asp*

the option of undoing them so you can try again. Throughout the process, a playback facility will let you listen to the changes you make, either on headphones or through monitor speakers.

Once you're happy with the results, you'll be able to save your work, but make sure whatever software you use is able to create WAV (PC) or AIFF (Mac) files, so you can process them in another application, or burn them to CD, in the best possible quality. If you're on a budget, and decide to go for free downloadable editing software,

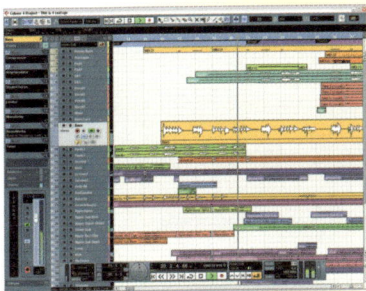

you'll find plenty available, but some will only export in MP3 format.

Finally, if you intend to upload your music to a website, or MySpace page, check to see whether the software you're considering is able to produce streaming audio files.

● ●
▲ *You'll be able to change the smallest detail on software such as Cubase.*

Mixers & Jukebox Software

4

Once you've added all the different instruments and effects to your multitrack recording, the next step is to create the two-channel stereo image that people will hear when they play your CD or download your music from the Internet. This process is known as mixing, and chances are you'll be doing it via your sequencing software package.

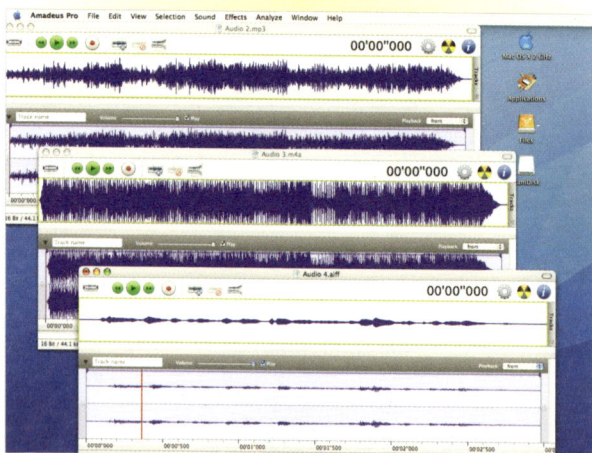

Most sequencing software includes programmes that allow you to take your multitrack recordings and combine the different elements to create a final stereo mix. During the mixing process you'll be able to change the volume of individual tracks relative to the others and move instruments to particular positions in the stereo field, or have them pan across from speaker to speaker. You could position the individual instruments to match your usual stage set-up, for example, or to highlight solos or backing vocals. You can use double-tracking and offsetting to give the final recording greater depth.

If your sequencer doesn't include mixing software, there are a number of separate programmes you can use. If you're using a Mac, try the pre-loaded GarageBand software, or download Audacity (freeware) or Amadeus (shareware). Audacity will also run on Windows systems, where you could also try MixPad (shareware).

••

◄ *If your sequencer does not include mixing software you will need a separate programme such as Amadeus.*

4

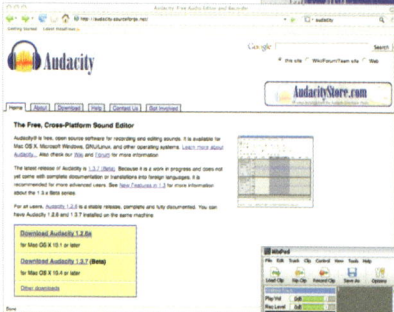

▶ *Audacity is free, open-source software for recording and editing sounds.*

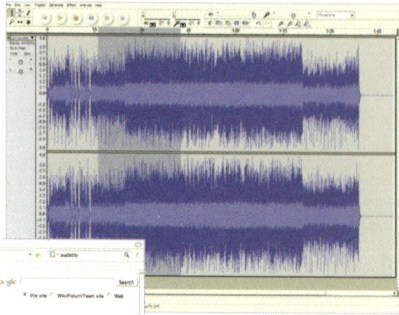

◀ *Download Audacity for free from http:// audacity.sourceforge.net*

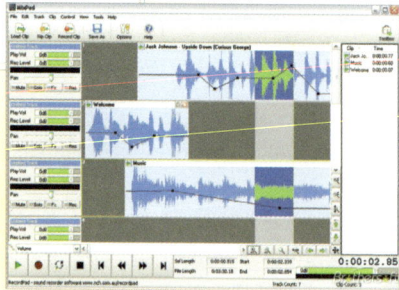

▶ *Mixing software such as MixPad is the digital replacement of using a multitrack recorder and mixing desk.*

It's worth noting that you need to use dedicated audio mixing software to produce your stereo masters. This needs to be able to import and process your multitrack recordings – DJ mixing software, which is often combined with jukebox software, is a completely different concept, designed to allow two (or more) different stereo recordings to be used to create a DJ mix.

Graphic Equalizers

Equalizers are one of the most common tools we have for processing audio. The bass and treble controls on your CD or MP3 player, a TV's tone control, a car stereo's loudness button and the graphic equalizer on a stereo system are all examples.

▲ *This car stereo is an example of a graphic equalizer.*

▼ *A graphic equalizer allows you to boost or cut a specified number of fixed frequency bands. A seven-band equalizer is shown. Using more bands gives you finer control over the EQ.*

In the studio, equalization, or EQ for short, is used on a recording to boost certain frequencies and cut others. By doing so you can compensate either for the acoustics of the room you record in, or for audio imperfections introduced when using microphones or other analogue gear. You might have two microphones that respond differently to higher or lower frequencies. Equalization is the key to making everything sound smooth and consistent.

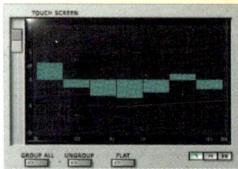

As well as applying equalization to individual channels prior to mixing, you can also use a graphic equalizer to make final adjustments to the overall sound of your recording. A graphic equalizer will typically have a bank of sliders, each capable of boosting or cutting a narrow range of frequencies, allowing you to make subtle improvements to the 'feel' of the final mix.

▶ *Performers use EQ to improve parts of their recording once it is completed.*

Almost all sequencing packages include a software graphic equalizer, but if yours doesn't there are plenty of free downloads available. Applying EQ is a skill worth working on – used carefully, equalization will give your recordings a professional finish that will make them stand out from the crowd.

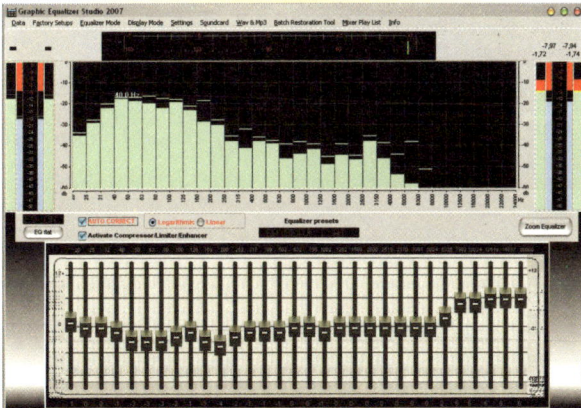

▲ *Graphic equalizers allow the user to control a number of different frequency bands in a stereophonic system.*

Online Sample Banks

Once you start recording and mixing your own music, it's likely that sooner or later you'll find yourself wanting to use a particular instrument or sound effect you don't already have in your arsenal.

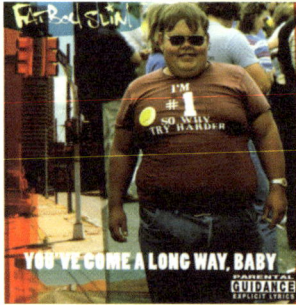

One of the great things about digital audio is that it makes it easy to store and share samples of just about any sound you can imagine. Whether it's a vintage keyboard, a hard-to-find percussion instrument or a short section of dialogue from a famous speech or film, it's likely that someone somewhere has exactly what you're looking for and you'll be able to find it online.

▲ *Fatboy Slim is known for the use of samples in his music.*

◄ *There are samples of all sorts of sound effects available online; for example, a didgeridoo.*

Many sites offer free audio samples for you to download and use as you wish, and there's a wide range to choose from. You'll need to be selective about the samples you download and use, though, because not only are many of them generic, sound quality is often an issue. If you're using free downloaded samples alongside

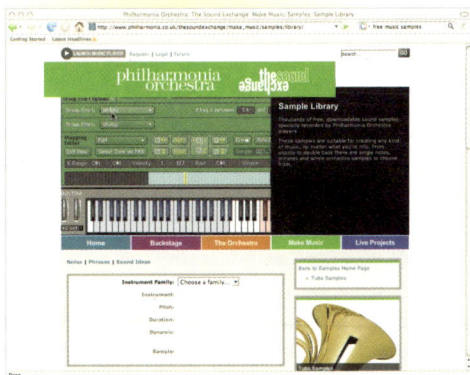

▲ *Thousands of free, downloadable sound samples specially recorded by Philharmonic Orchestra players are available from www.philharmonia.co.uk*

professionally recorded ones you'll need to make sure they don't stick out like the proverbial sore thumb.

Alongside the freebies, a lot of sites also sell CDs of top-quality samples, and these are definitely worth considering. In the long run, spending a few pounds on professional-quality samples may make all the difference when people listen to your demo or decide whether to buy your album.

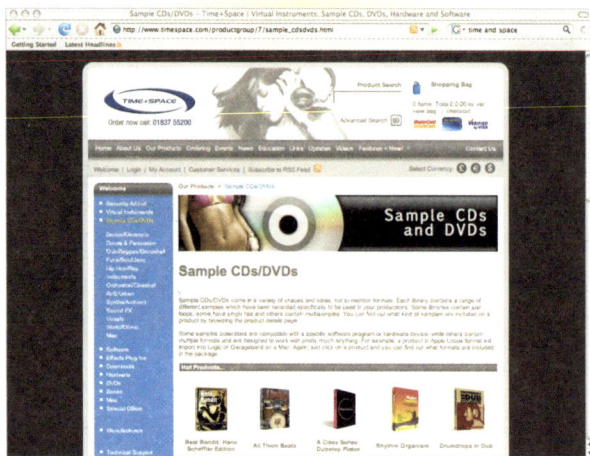

▲ It may be worth spending a bit of money on top-quality samples. Sites such as www.timespace.com sell CDs of audio samples.

Free Software On The Web

In home recording, as in everything you do on a computer, finding the right software can be a headache, especially if you're on a tight budget. You can spend hundreds of pounds on software, but if you don't have any previous experience choosing the programmes that are right for you can be difficult.

Fortunately, there are many cheaper options to explore.

There are several websites offering links to hundreds of free downloadable software packages that will cover everything you need to get started in your home studio. Not only that, but there are dozens of discussion groups and forums where you can find advice and opinions to help you choose the set-up that's best suited to your needs.

Apple Macintosh users are lucky to have GarageBand, pre-loaded on almost all Macs sold in the past few years, and a very good audio editing and mastering package for those taking their first steps on the road to fame and fortune. The Garage Door (http://www.thegaragedoor.com/) started out as a site dedicated to GarageBand, but now carries lots of news and reviews related to every aspect of home recording.

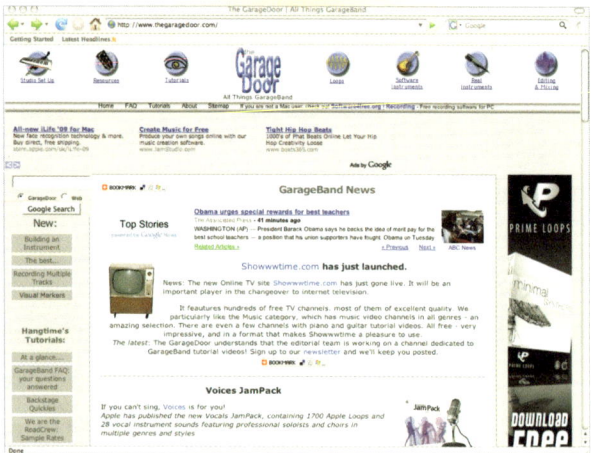

For Windows and Linux users, there are other places to look – the Hitsquad Musicians Network (http://www.hitsquad.com/smm/freeware/),

◀ *www.thegaragedoor.com is a site dedicated to GarageBand.*

Freebytes (http://www.freebyte.com/music_software/),
Software4free (http://www.software4free.org/recording.html), Free Music Software, (http://freemusic
software.org/category/free-audio-software) all offer
links to a huge range of free software for just about
any recording or mastering application, while Home
Recording Connection (http://www.homerecording
connection.com/links.php) has links to both freeware
and other items of interest, including studio
equipment, recording guides and music biz
information. There's more advice available at
http://homerecording.about.com/

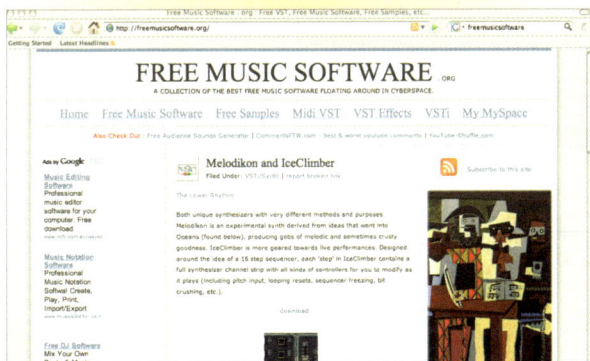

▲ *www.freemusicsoftware.org does what it says on the tin!*

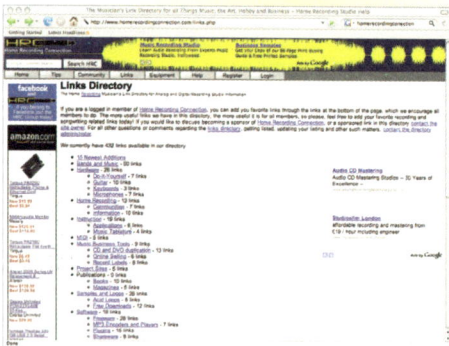

◄ *Top: www.hitsquad.com has links to freeware on the web.*

◄ *Centre: download a range of software at www.freebyte.com*

◄ *Bottom: www.homerecordingconnection.com has links to freeware and other items of interest.*

If you're thinking of buying one of the commercially available packages, remember that you can sometimes try them out for free by downloading an evaluation copy. These will be fully functional, but work for a limited period only – normally 30 days, so make sure you're set up and ready to go before you download. In other cases, a free downloadable version of the software might be available, offering only some of the functionality of the full, commercially available version.

HANDY HINTS

Keep up with all the latest studio developments by checking out online magazines such as
Sound on Sound (www.soundonsound.com),
Tape Op (www.tapeop.com),
Audio Media (www.audiomedia.com)
and *Recording* (www.recordingmag.com).

Summary

Check your progress against this list

Check the compatibility of everything
you acquire – both hardware and software ...... ☐

Check which computers have the
best reputation among music-makers........... ☐

Consider going with computer-bundled software
to 'learn the ropes' before splashing out........... ☐

Ask advice if you need it – and even
if you think you don't .... ☐

Check out the home recording websites
listed for up-to-date information................ ☐

Always have your final aim in mind.
Don't over-complicate .... ☐

Don't forget physical needs such as
microphone stands, pop filters and cables .... ☐

Make sure a circuit-breaker protects
your expensive computer equipment .... ☐

Use websites and Internet forums to keep
up with the latest developments and options ... ☐

USING DIGITAL MUSIC FILES

Introduction

The digital music revolution has made buying, storing, creating and manipulating music immeasurably easier – but it has also given rise to a vast number of acronyms and technical terms that are guaranteed to confuse the issue. Here we look at the different types of file format, where they can be obtained and how to change between and store them. Once mastered, these basic skills will leave you better equipped to make the most of the technology and become a master of the digital realm. Vive la revolution!

Downloading Music From The Web

Obtaining music from the Internet and storing it on your computer so you can play it again and again is known as downloading, as opposed to music you can access through your computer from radio stations or jukeboxes, which is known as streaming. There are also peer-to-peer networks allowing file-sharing, but these are not always legal.

HANDY HINTS

Free music is obtainable legally from certain up-and-coming artists – but they will clearly state this. Check out websites like MP3.com, yahoo.com and lycos.com

▶ *Once you have downloaded a song on to your computer you can then put it on to your portable music player.*

158

5

HANDY HINTS

Two of the most popularly downloaded
file formats, MP3 or WMA (Windows Media
Audio), can be played on all PCs thanks to
Windows Media Player. Click the Start button,
then go to *Programmes*, then *Accessories*,
then *Entertainment*, where you click on
Windows Media Player.

Not all the audio formats used will be compatible with every music player or computer, though the most popular current sound file format, MP3, works on both Mac and PCs. Other file formats include AIFF (for Mac); AU for Mac and UNIX; WAV for the PC; and RA for Real Audio, a proprietary system for delivering and playing streaming audio on the web. These are discussed in more detail elsewhere in this book.

Some online music stores are independent of computer operating systems, while others require the use of Microsoft Windows to utilize their software. The use of Digital Rights Management, which restricts

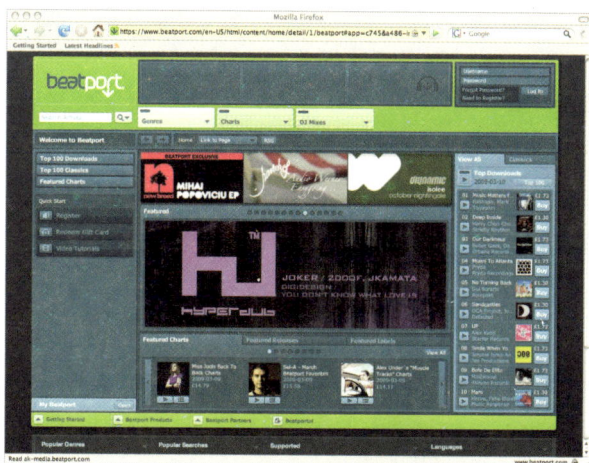

▼ *There are specialist online music stores such as www.beatport.com, which sells electronic dance music downloads.*

making extra copies of the music or limits its use on certain devices, is now largely being abandoned.

In addition to music stores, peer-to-peer downloading programmes or websites are very popular; torrent file-sharing is a common method of peer-to-peer transfers, but there is much controversy relating to

◄ *iTunes is the most well-known online music store. You can download individual tracks or a whole album.*

sharing files in this way due to copyright matters. Even so, it dwarfs the online retail sector: in 2006, an estimated five billion songs were swapped on peer-to-peer websites globally, compared to 509 million purchased online.

Downloading is here to stay, as was proved in November 2005 when Gwen Stefani's 'Hollaback Girl' passed the one million downloads mark, making it the first song to achieve 'diamond' download status.

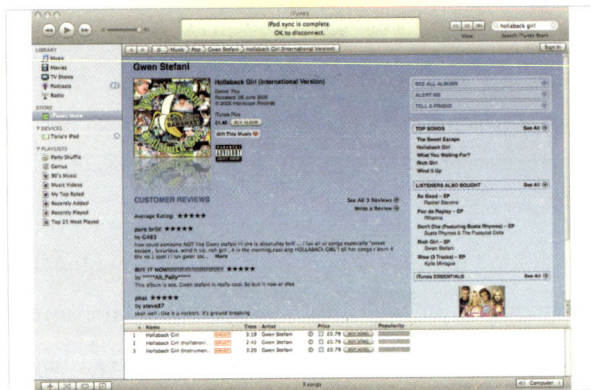

▲ *Gwen Stefani's single 'Hollaback Girl' was the first to achieve 'diamond' download status in 2005.*

File Formats Explained

When you're working with digital audio, you'll be dealing with a wide range of file formats. Many of these are directly related to the software used to create them. A lot of the time, you won't need to worry about formats unless you're planning to use data created in one application as input to another. Even then, most applications will allow you to save your work as a WAV or AIFF file – standard formats that can be imported into most audio software.

File formats become much more important when you're saving and storing your music. There are a number of audio file formats, and almost all of them compress the data in some way to reduce the space needed to store them. There are two types of audio compression – lossless and lossy – and advantages and disadvantages to each.

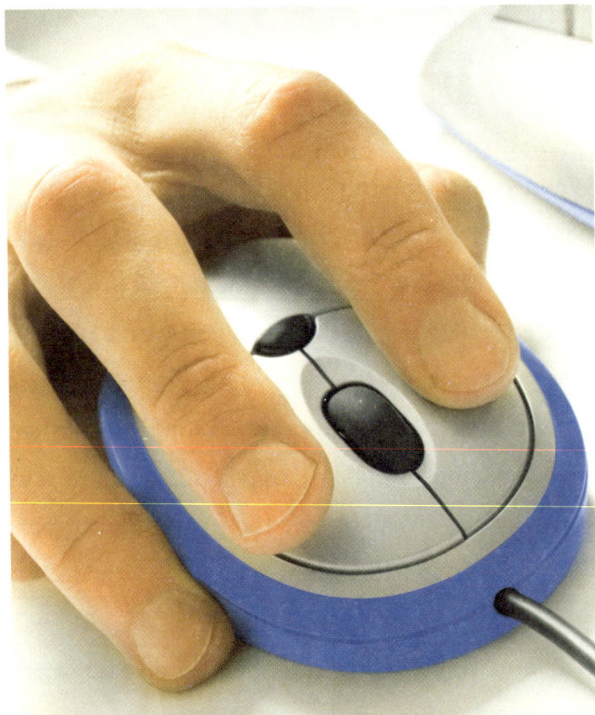

▼ *File formats are important when you save and store your music.*

HANDY HINTS

Make a note of which file formats work with
your computer operating system and which
do not. It could save expensive mistakes.

Lossless compression saves an exact copy of the original audio and allows you to reconstruct it from the compressed file. WAV, AIFF, SHN and FLAC files are all examples of audio files created using lossless compression.

Lossy compression creates a much smaller file, but as the name suggests some of the original audio data is discarded when the copy is created, so you lose quality. MP3 files are the most common example of lossy compression – the highest and lowest frequencies are stripped out, along with selected frequencies in between, drastically reducing the space needed to store the files.

▲ *MP3 files are the most common example of lossy compression.*

It's essential to save master copies of your music in a lossless format – you can run off CD-quality copies if you need them, or convert to streaming audio or MP3 format for online distribution. Keep your options open – remember, once a file is encoded to MP3, the discarded data is gone forever. You can convert MP3 files back to WAV or AIFF, but this won't restore the missing data – all you'll be doing is creating a bigger file with the same reduced sound quality.

▲ *It is essential to save CD-quality master copies of your music in a lossless format.*

Changing Between Formats

Converting files from one format to another is an essential part of working with digital audio. As we've seen, different applications store and work with digital audio data in different ways, often using their own file formats to do so. Most applications will allow you to save or export audio data in a number of standard formats, but sometimes you'll still need to convert files, so you'll need some file conversion software.

Most DAW software includes a conversion programme, but if you need a stand-alone converter make sure

▶ *Converting files from one format to another is an essential part of working with digital audio.*

▼ *Switch enables you to convert a file into many different formats.*

you find one that will handle all the commonly used formats. You can buy file conversion software, but there's really no need — there are dozens of free downloadable programmes that will do the job, including Switch, dBpowerAmp and Audacity, so take a look online and check out what's on offer.

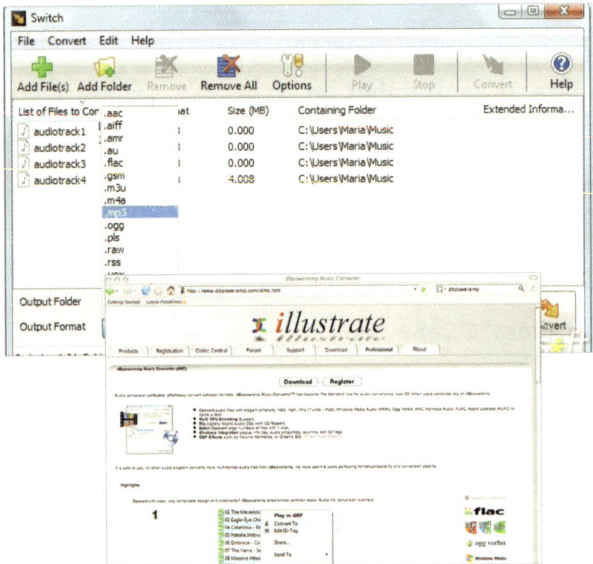

▲ *Download dBpowerAmp conversion software from www.dbpoweramp.com*

If you want to create streaming audio for your website, you'll need a separate programme to reformat and upload the files. How you create and upload your content depends on the platform you're using (Windows for PC, OS X for Mac, etc.), so you'll need to look for the software that's appropriate. Among the free programmes available to create streaming audio content are Windows Media Encoder 7, Helix Producer (creates Real Audio format) and Autodesk Cleaner Basic (for Mac).

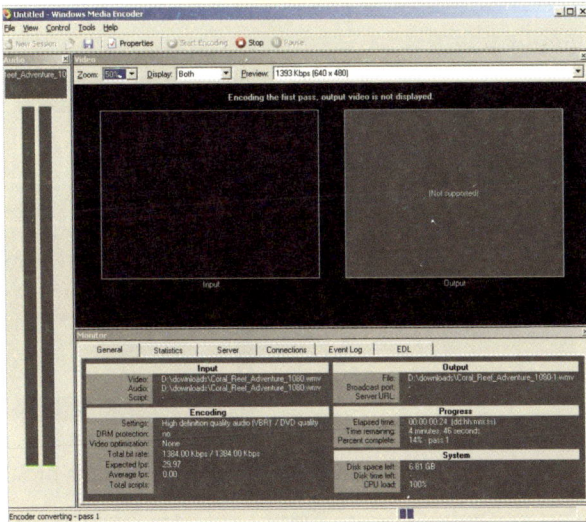

▲ *Among the free programmes available to create streaming audio content is Windows Media Encoder.*

Using Memory Cards

The use of memory cards for storing audio files has seen a rapid expansion in the past few years. Memory cards first appeared in the early 1990s, and were originally intended to provide additional plug-in PC memory, but they quickly found their way into games consoles, digital cameras and mobile phones.

It's taken a while for memory cards to gain a foothold in the recording studio, but in the past five years a number of digital recording devices have been introduced that allow you to store audio data on Compact Flash or SD (Secure Digital) cards. These cards are inexpensive, widely available and offer a number of advantages over other storage methods.

• •

◄ *This is a Secure Digital memory card. Even 1GB will give you around 40 minutes of eight-track recording.*

Unlike a hard drive, they can be removed from the recorder, allowing recordings to be transported easily from location to location. They're solid state, making them physically robust and better able to preserve and protect your data. Compact Flash and SD are internationally recognized standard formats, so you can use them in any device with a memory card reader. Card readers in computers and mobile phones give you even more opportunities for distributing your music to everyone from record labels to family and friends.

• • • • • • • • • • • • • • • • • • • •

► *Memory cards are easily transported from place to place.*

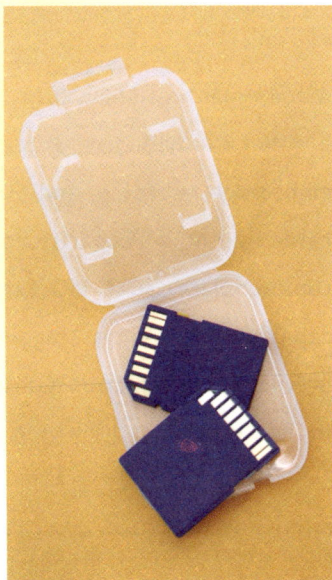

▼ *You can use memory cards in any device with a memory card reader. Or you can attach an external memory card reader.*

Memory cards can hold large quantities of data – even a 1GB card will give you around 40 minutes of eight-track recording, and SDHC (SD High Capacity) cards with a capacity of 32GB are already commonplace. SDXC (SD Extended Capacity) cards, capable of holding a staggering 2TB of data, were previewed at the 2009 Consumer Electronics Show in Las Vegas.

▶ *Use a memory card to back up your tracks at regular intervals.*

HANDY HINTS

Shop around for memory cards. Sometimes, you'll find that buying a package with two 2GB cards is cheaper than buying one 4GB card. As with anything you buy studio-wise, do a little comparison shopping before making your final purchase.

Perhaps the best way in which you can use a memory card is to back up your tracks at regular intervals. It avoids the painful possibility of losing the product of days of work through accident – something that, once experienced, you will not want to repeat.

Summary

Check your progress against this list

Be aware that, while compact and handy,
MP3 loses detail to make its file size small ...... ☐

WAV and AIFF formats are universally
recognized by PC and Mac respectively .... ☐

Always save your music in a lossless format .... ☐

Find free file conversion software before
you need it .... ☐

Consider streaming songs from your website
rather than offering downloads .... ☐

Keep a crib sheet of acronyms so you
don't get confused by too many initials......... ☐

Back your work up regularly on to Compact
Flash or SD (Secure Digital) memory cards ...... ☐

Keep spare memory cards handy
in case of emergency........................... ☐

PROMOTING & SELLING YOUR MUSIC

It's not enough to make great music – you have to make people aware of it. The Internet is the most powerful tool you can use in your quest to get your band and music known. Its alternative name, the World Wide Web, reminds us that it covers the globe, so the possibilities are limitless. If you make a fan on a remote Pacific island they can now access and download your music to enjoy, even though you may never meet! And it's all possible for the cost of an Internet subscription – so what are you waiting for?

SOCIAL NETWORKING SITES

Introduction

The two ways to make yourself known via the Internet are creating a website and joining online communities. If you don't want to build a website straight away, sites like MySpace will let you create a web presence in an afternoon. And once you have a site, blogs (online diaries) and even the humble email are among the ways to keep your fans informed and spread the word to new ones.

Distributing your music can be done on the physical and digital levels: most successful bands use a combination. But thinking 'outside the box' often pays dividends.

What Is Social Networking?

Social networking is a way to communicate and share information using the World Wide Web. It began in the mid-1990s as a niche activity, but really took off in the 2000s when the computer found a place in homes and Internet access became the rule rather than the exception. The first such site was Friendster, and now, thanks to the popularity of MySpace, Facebook, Bebo and others, it seems that social networking will be an enduring

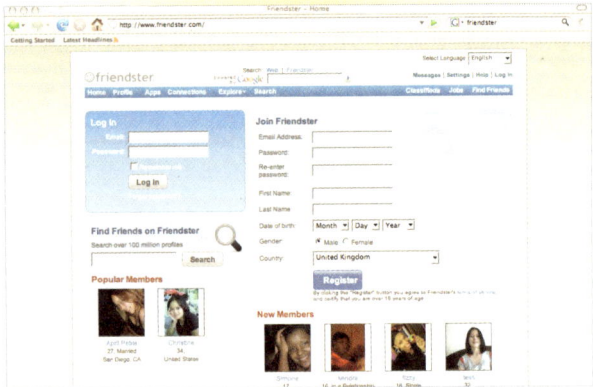

▲ *Friendster was the first online social network.*

part of everyday life. MySpace, with over 100 million accounts, has become the digital equivalent of hanging out at the shopping mall as teenagers load their profiles with photos, news about music and details of their likes and dislikes.

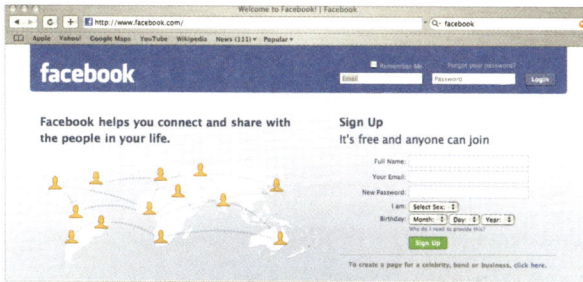

▲▼ *Facebook, MySpace, Bebo and others have millions of users worldwide.*

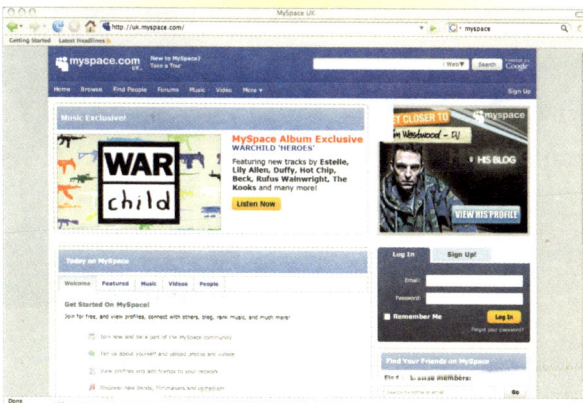

These sites are online places where users can create their own profile and build a personal network that connects him or her to other users. Many users share interests and/or activities, such as music. Most social network services are web-based and offer a variety of ways for users to interact, such as email and instant messaging.

In the past five years, social networking has become a phenomenon that engages tens of millions of Internet users, the majority of them young: a 2007 survey found that over half (55 per cent) of all online American youths between the ages of 12 and 17 use online social networking sites, and the picture is likely to be the same in the UK. Bebo trails behind MySpace and Facebook in the United States in terms of traffic, but is the most popular social networking site in the United Kingdom.

▲ *A survey found that over half of all online American youths between then ages of 12 and 17 use online social networking sites.*

How Do Social Networking Sites Work?

The first thing you have to do, clearly, is sign up. This is invariably free of charge. To edit information on your account, you have to log in or provide an access code. This prevents unauthorized users from posting pictures and editing personal information without your permission.

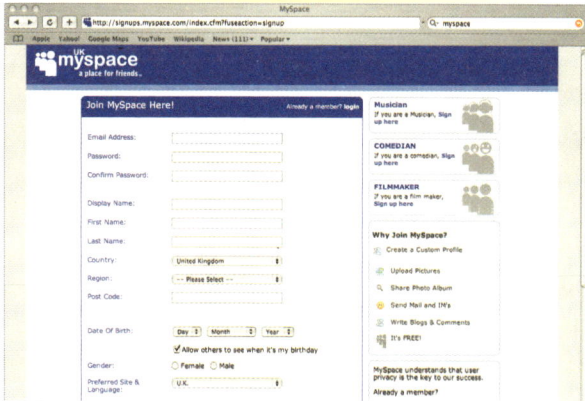

▲ *The first thing you have to do is sign up!*

When you join a social networking site you will be prompted to choose a screen name and create a profile containing personal information including your age, home town, school/college, likes and dislikes. Come up with a user name and password before you start and write them down in case of temporary amnesia!

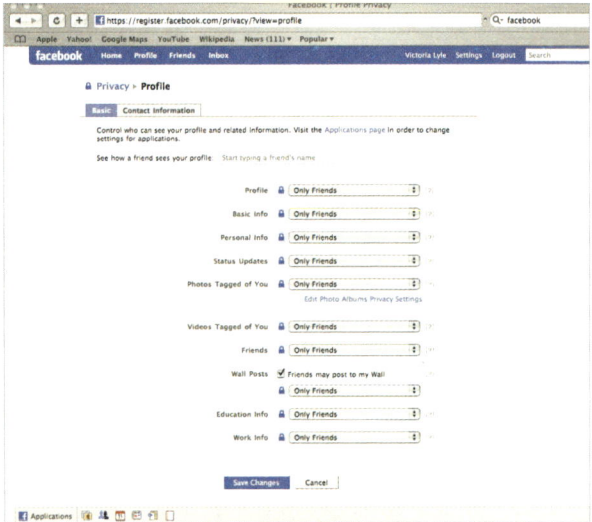

▲ *If 'only friends' can view your profile then it will be more difficult to reach as many people as possible. If you are worried about privacy, have a personal account that is private and a band account that the public can look at.*

▼ *Once you have set up your profile page customize it with music, pictures and information.*

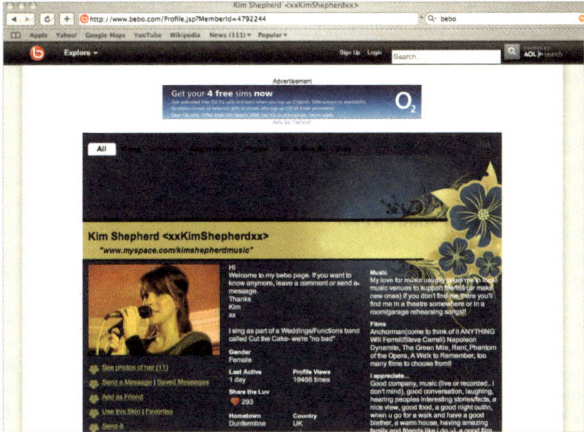

Many social networking sites let the user choose who can view their profile, preventing unauthorized users from accessing their information. (Clearly, if you want to reach as many people as possible, you should choose the 'public view' option.)

Having joined and set up a profile page, you'll need to customize it with music, pictures and information. You can then invite friends to your site to post comments. People can apply to be your friends and you can approve them or not.

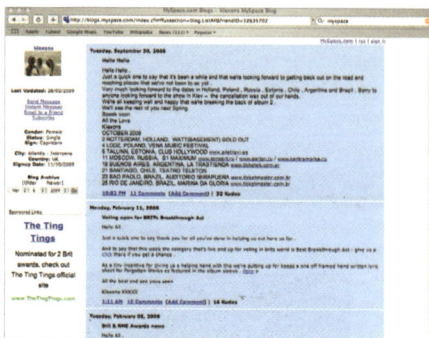

▶ *Use your blog to let your fans know what you have been up to and what your plans are for the future.*

You can create blog pages letting people know what you have been up to and what your future plans are. This feature is like an online diary. An audio blog is called a Podcast, and can often be downloaded and played on an iPod or MP3 player.

Once you have your profile page up and running, let everyone know about it by including the address on emails, press releases, CDs and everything you produce.

HANDY HINTS

Be very suspicious if a screen mentions money and, as always with the Internet, do not disclose any financial details like bank account numbers.

How Can They Help Promote My Music?

You now have the ability to upload video footage of yourself and your band mates and expose it to an unlimited number of potential fans. In the UK Sandi Thom went from unknown singer-songwriter to chart-topper by broadcasting mini-gigs from her South London basement flat to the world, while US teen sensations the Jonas Brothers traded on their good looks and wacky sense of humour by posting home videos of their crazy life and times.

▶ The Jonas Brothers gained popularity by posting videos on sites such as YouTube.

If you can get a celebrity blogger to talk about you then your fame will spread like wildfire. Perez Hilton, the well known American blogger, attracts upwards of four million viewers per day to his site, PerezHilton.com – but even if you can't get him to notice you there are other possibilities closer to home. The *Sun*, Britain's leading tabloid newspaper, has the-sun.co.uk, while other gossip pages of note include tmz.com and mrpaparazzi.com

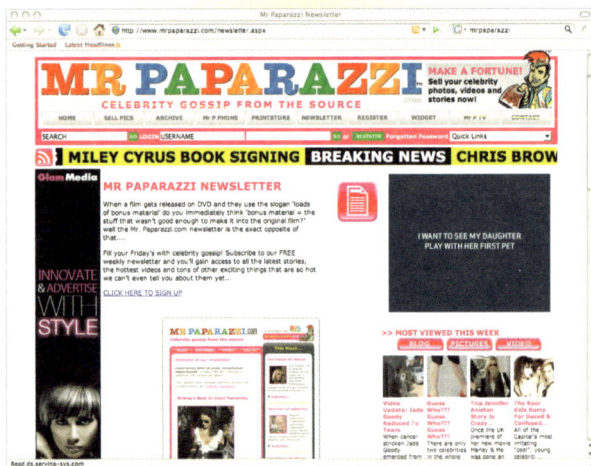

▲ *If you can get on to celebrity gossip websites, such as www.mrpaparazzi.com, your fame will spread rapidly.*

▼ *American blogger Perez Hilton attracts upwards of four million viewers to his site per day.*

The Arctic Monkeys and Lily Allen are among the successful UK stars whose clever use of the Internet meant there was a huge demand for their music even before they had officially released anything. We continue by giving you advice tailored specifically to the social networking sites you may wish to investigate. There are concepts such as friends, subscriptions, flyers and Bebo's oddly titled 'Become a Groupie' function. So there's plenty for your fans to enjoy once you are up and running.

▼ *Lily Allen used social networking sites to create interest and demand for her music before she had released anything.*

It's not all about publicity, of course. You can also sell music and merchandise via the Internet, but the main use of social networking sites is to create a buzz about yourselves by clever use of music, video and other incentives to catch your fans and reel them in. You should soon see the result in gig attendances, and when you're playing sellout club shows you'll be ready to progress to the next level.

Using MySpace

Using MySpace to promote music took off in a big way in 2006 when Lily Allen built up her online presence as she prepared to release her first single. Her music has been downloaded from her site over 19 million times, and with 445,000 friends she was the fifth most popular musical act of 2008.

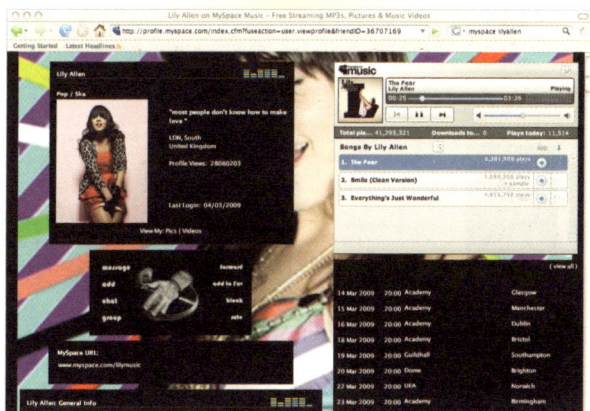

Short of having your own dedicated band website – and of course you can have both – MySpace is arguably the best social networking tool to promote your band,

▲ *Lily Allen used MySpace to build up her online presence.*

▼ *Many bands have a website and a MySpace page.*

whether signed or unsigned. It offers the opportunity to upload and display photos and videos, a MySpace blog and bulletins to get news to fans and friends and, most importantly, the facility to upload MP3s to your MySpace page's music player.

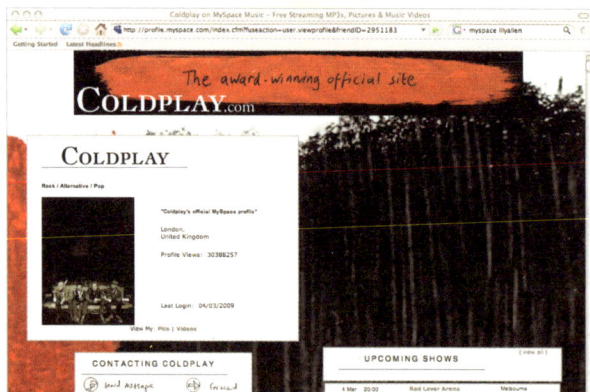

HANDY HINTS

If you opt for a MySpace page, try messaging bands who play a similar style of music and offer an exchange, of sorts, by putting them in your 'top 8' that is displayed in your front page for a week if they do the same.

▼ *Get creative with the layout of your MySpace page.*

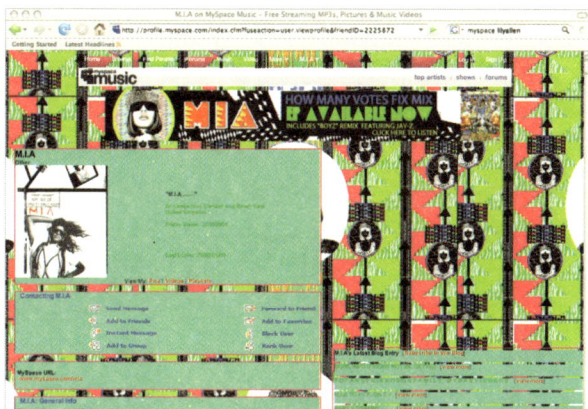

MySpace allows you to be pretty creative with the layout of your page, with the option to choose from some pre-designed layouts or, when editing your page's info, to put in your own HTML and customize it to fit your band's image.

HANDY HINTS

If you are on a line-up for a show with other bands, put them all in your MySpace top 8 and vice versa. Who knows how many extra fans you could each pick up and attract to the gig if you are displayed on other bands' front pages?

MySpace Help

Even if you aren't well versed in HTML (of which you will read more later), there are loads of sites that can help offering hundreds of different layouts; with the help of 'generators', you can input your desired colours and preferences and the website will generate HTML code for you to put on your page.

Try these sites:

☆ http://www.mygen.co.uk

☆ http://www.myspacemaster.net

☆ http://www.mylayoutscreator.com

☆ http://www.layoutgeneratormyspace.com

☆ http://my-spacelayouts.co.uk

HANDY HINTS

Use the diversity of MySpace, which now has MySpace Music, MySpace TV (a competitor to YouTube), MySpace karaoke (self explanatory) and many other offshoots.

The original MySpace was founded in 2003 as a looser, music-driven version of pioneering social networking site Friendster. Its membership of mostly teens and twenty-somethings grew rapidly to some 185 million users, making it one of the Internet's most popular websites. In 2005 News Corp paid $580 million to buy Intermix Media, MySpace's former parent company.

● ●
▲ *Sites such as www.myspacemaster.net offer lots of different layouts for your MySpace page.*

Using YouTube

Someone called YouTube 'the next generation's MTV'. And just as MTV revolutionized music television as the world woke up to satellite and cable television, so YouTube is the most popular way to see bands today. The big difference is that YouTube is accessible to all.

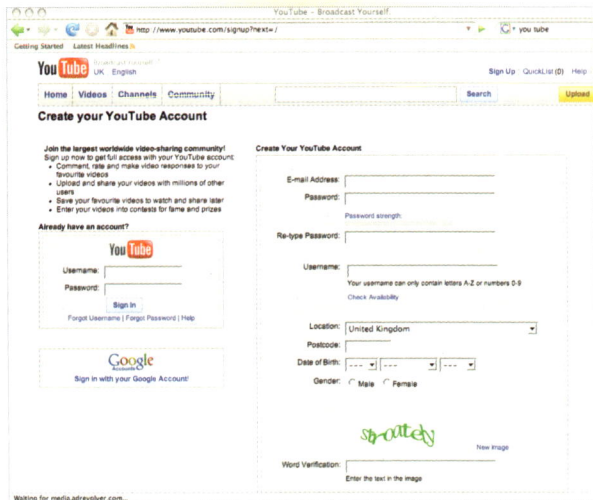

▲ *It is easy and free to sign up to YouTube.*

▼ *YouTube's playback technology allows viewers to see top-quality videos of their favourite bands.*

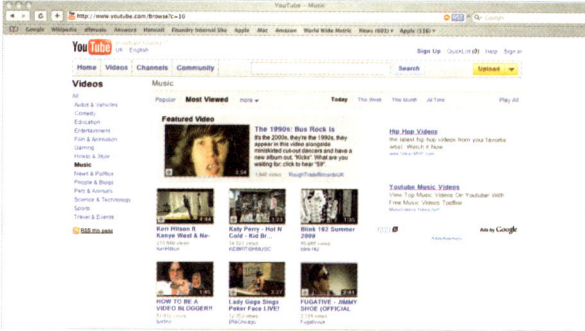

Three former PayPal employees created YouTube in February 2005. In November 2006, the company was bought by Google for $1.65 billion, and it is now operated as a subsidiary of Google. Its video playback technology for web users is based on the Adobe Flash Player and allows the site to display videos with a quality comparable to more established video playback technologies, such as Windows Media Player, QuickTime and RealPlayer, that require the user to download and install a web browser plug-in. YouTube does not, however, offer a download link for its videos, so it is strictly 'view only'.

▼ *YouTube is a great way to showcase your visual and audio appeal.*

It is a great tool for bands and singers, giving the opportunity to showcase your visual and audio appeal by hosting videos. When you've set up an account, (the registration form is simple and accessible via the 'sign up' function on the home

HANDY HINTS

YouTube videos generate a url/http address for easy sharing and an HTML code that can be used to embed it on social networking pages.

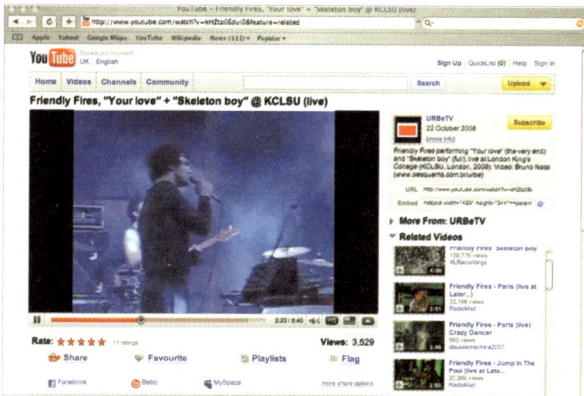

page, and registration is free) viewers can 'subscribe' to your channel, getting emails and updates on their YouTube home page to alert them to new videos. Comments on videos give instant feedback and it's easy to track hits/views of the video to monitor your (hopefully fast-growing) popularity.

Fans can post video responses – but be prepared for criticism as well as praise, it comes with the territory. Tagging videos with keywords, the more the better, will ensure your offering is easier to be found on the YouTube video search.

▲ *You can upload videos of your gigs and even receive video responses from fans.*

At the end of the day, appearing on YouTube is no guarantee of popularity – you have to have the raw talent and strike lucky with who sees it. But as a way of exposing your stage act to fans and potential fans it cannot be beaten.

▲ *Fans can comment on your videos. Be prepared for criticism as well as praise.*

HANDY HINTS

YouTube awards daily rankings for popular videos, so if you get your fans motivated you could find yourself a place in the charts.

Using Facebook

The 70 million member network known as Facebook is currently the trendiest social networking site. It is less customizable than some rivals but offers the functions of groups (where you can chat on the 'wall', have discussions, upload pictures and videos and directly message your members).

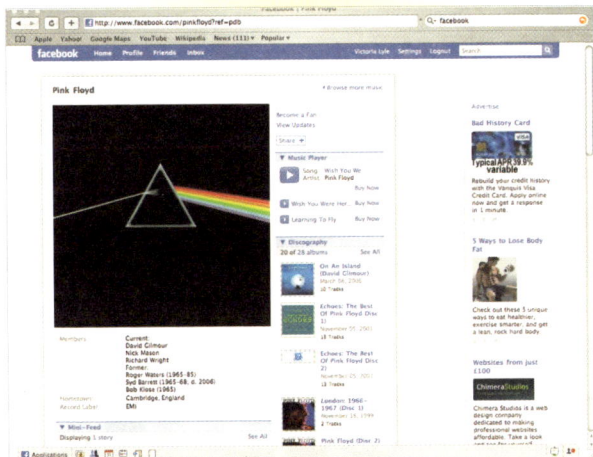

6

▲ *Both established and up-and-coming bands have Facebook pages.*

It also offers the fun function to create fan pages where Facebookers can become a 'fan of' your band. With Facebook's 'news feed' displaying your Facebookers' friends' recent activity, it is easy for people to see someone become a fan or join a fan group and they may be inclined to investigate further. Members can also invite friends to join groups, which opens up many different promotion possibilities.

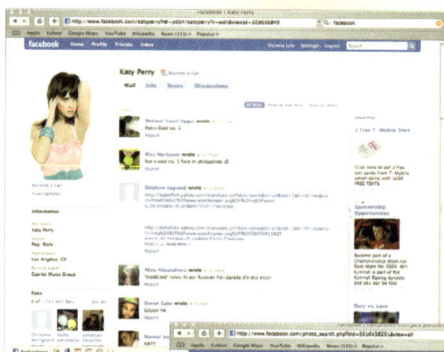

◄ *Fans can write comments on your wall.*

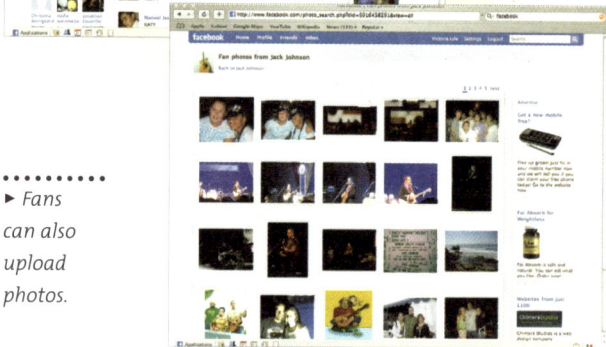

► *Fans can also upload photos.*

You can get the ball rolling by sending event invites from your band's page and track acceptances. These can get spread virally to your friends' friends; every show you do should be promoted with one of these.

The greatest benefit to having a Facebook group is that you will have a direct link from every member's profile. The more members you have the more links to your group will be out there. It's an exponential thing because, as you gain more members, more may well follow.

Applications can be created that will play one of your band's songs or syndicate your band's blog (if your band doesn't have a blog, it should!). People love to send their friends cool new 'apps', so take advantage and you could soon be seeing a lot of new Facebook faces at your shows.

HANDY HINTS

Beware of blogging first and thinking afterwards. Even if you think better of an entry and delete it, there's no guarantee it hasn't been archived somewhere on the web!

Using Bebo

Social networking site Bebo, recently acquired by AOL for $850 million, has 43 million users and at the time of writing is claimed to be the United Kingdom's most popular social networking site.

When you set up your Bebo profile, it is automatically deemed to be 'private', in other words accessible only to your friends. But this is somewhat self-defeating for

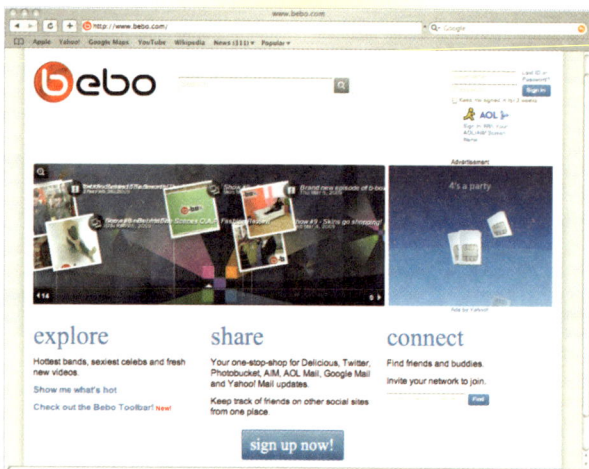

▲ *'Bebo' is an acronym for 'Blog early, blog often'.*

publicity-seeking purposes, so you will undoubtedly wish to select the Public Profile option, which will allow all members to see what you are posting.

The most useful aspect of Bebo for musicians is Bebo Music, launched in 2006, which encourages you to post details of musicians, tours and blogs. Lady Gaga is just

▲ *Like other social networking sites, on Bebo you can upload songs, videos and photos, write a blog and see fans' comments.*

one of many current stars who have tapped into the popularity of Bebo to build their profile and encourage demand for their music – even if it is, as yet, unreleased. Bands can upload an unlimited number of tracks – in contrast to MySpace, where you're limited – and has its own customizable profile at a clean URL (bandname.bebo.com), which can also feature tour dates and photos. Users can 'Become a Groupie' (adding a band to your friends list) and set up a

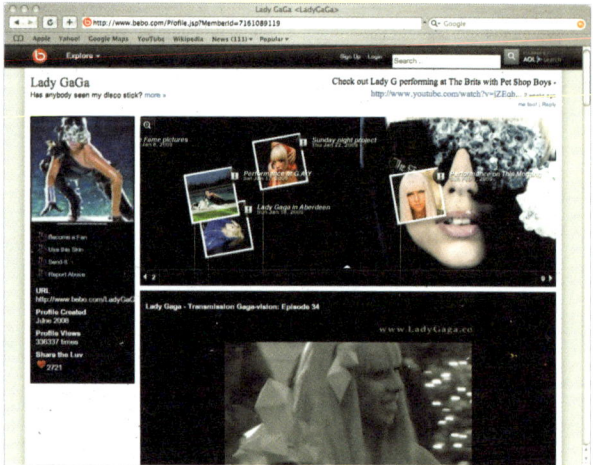

▲ *Lady Gaga used Bebo to build her profile and create demand for her music.*

playlist of favourite songs. Bebo aggregates the data in these lists to create a site-wide 'playlist chart'. The featured bands are skewed heavily towards the UK scene, reflecting Bebo's current dominance of the UK social networking market.

▲ *Bebo creates a music chart from all the songs fans have added to their playlists.*

Other Social Networking Sites

Twitter

Twitter is becoming very popular, notably with celebrities like Jonathan Ross and Lily Allen, whose comments are read by thousands. The concept is pretty much the same as the updating status feature of Facebook; telling people what you are doing on an hour-by-hour basis, it is a great way to be in touch with fans.

HANDY HINTS

Try Twittering – it's the latest buzz in social networking and looks set to be so for quite some time to come. Even the *Daily Mail* has heard of it!

It can be updated from web or phone, so celebs such as Lily Allen use it to regularly update fans when on tour and travelling. It also has a function to upload pictures (from phone or web) to share with 'followers'.

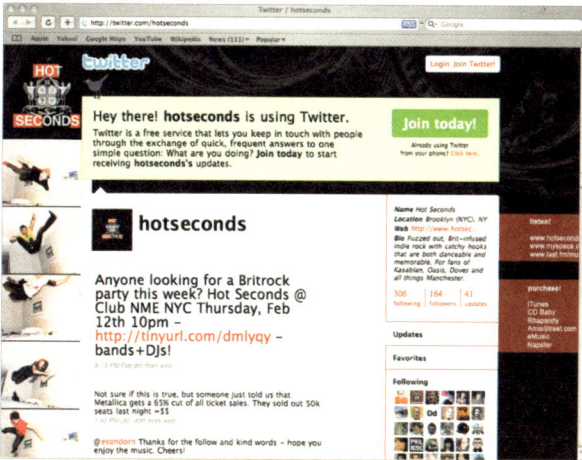

It works like a constant news feed, so you can 'follow' someone and read their updates. If that person follows you back ('follower') they will be able to read your 'tweets' (updates). People can reply to a Twitterer personally by directing their message at the person by including @username (e.g. @theband) in the message.

▲ *Use Twitter to announce your upcoming gigs.*

▼ *Respond personally to a Twitterer by writing '@username'.*

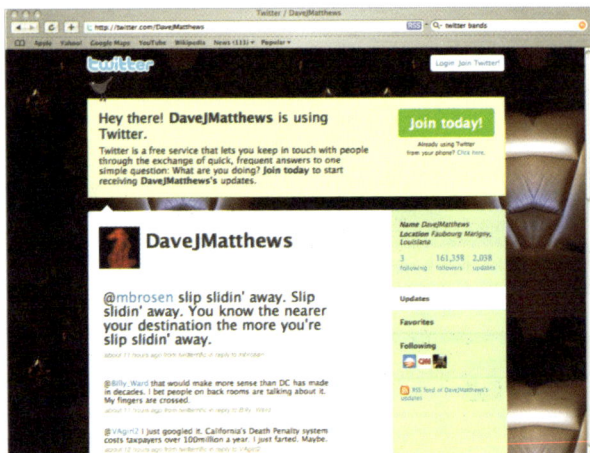

Last.fm

This online radio station allows you to create a band page with biography, and to upload music, etc. Users can add your band to their library of music. Last.fm has a download called Audioscrobbler that you can install, which tracks what music you listen to on the PC and can match you up with friends with similar music tastes – a great way to get into new music. (Example page: http://www.last.fm/music/You+Me+At+Six). On Last.fm you can also upload videos, link to stores where your music is available, and view charts by popularity.

▼ *Kings of Leon band pages on Last.fm. The tabs on the left-hand side take fans to different pages of their profile.*

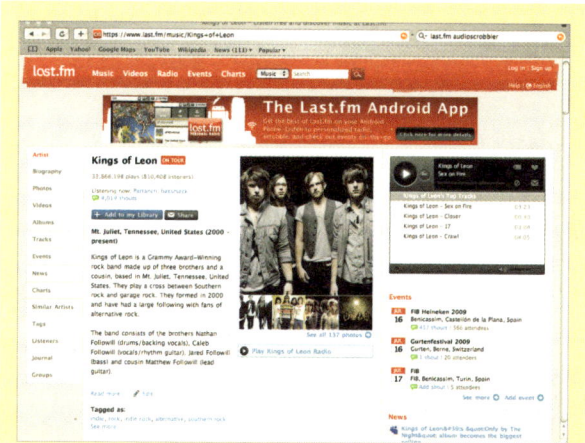

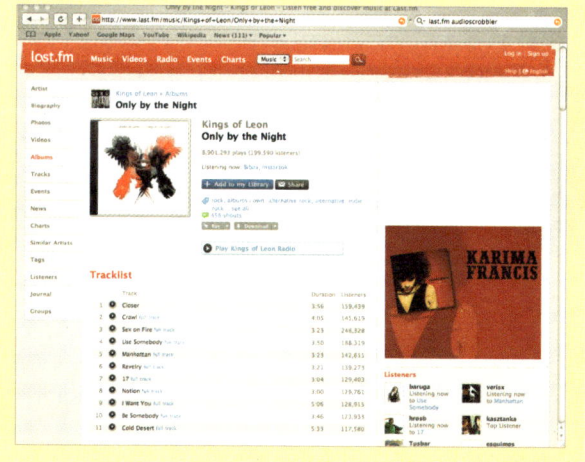

▲ *Fans can choose to buy, download or just listen to music by adding it to their library.*

Summary

Check your progress against this list

Join as many social networks as you
can – it's free!.................................. ☐

Write blogs (online diaries) to make
fans feel included.............................. ☐

Suggest links with other bands
in your field of music .... ☐

Feature your site address(es)
on everything you do .... ☐

Get on YouTube and use the footage
on your own sites and blogs .... ☐

See if you can get a celebrity blogger
to mention you for some real or
imaginary achievement....................... ☐

Make as many online friends as you can........ ☐

1
2
3
4
5
6
7
8
9
10
11
12

CREATING YOUR OWN WEBSITE

Introduction

Why do you want a website? To help you build a following? Get better-paid gigs? Impress your friends? Find a manager and/or get a record company deal? It's true a website can do any or all of these things, but how you do it and where you put it may be determined by the answers to some of those questions. If you are building a website from scratch and you haven't done it before then the easiest options are either to just do a MySpace page or Google 'website templates' and find a free ready-made shell you can copy and use as the basis of your site. We offer hints for more ambitious projects, but the main aim is to get a web presence – you can always improve it as you go.

What Makes A Good Website?

Being a band website, your content will be a mix of visual, audio and video – all things which take time to load, so you should have an attractive website that's not overly complicated or visitors will get bored and leave before it's even loaded.

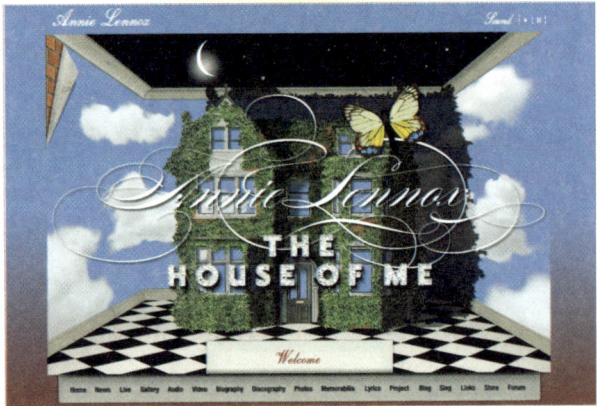

Avoid automatic music unless you want your visitor to be embarrassed at work and instantly close your website. Have music but make it optional. Have a 'play music' button, and advertise your sound samples well

▼ *Have music on your website, but make it optional.*

enough for people to choose to play them – don't stuff them down people's throats.

Who are you looking to impress? If you've sold out the top pub venue in your town on a regular basis, and the landlord says so in an endorsement, that means a great deal to another pub gig booker. If your main aim is building a following, you want your fans saying what a great time they had at your gig – then get them to say it again on your MySpace comments section, YouTube films, chat rooms, Facebook, etc., etc!

◄ *Your website should look good, but not be overly complicated.*

Website Format & Image

Always have a striking picture of the band – or the singer – on your home page. People will judge your entire band and everything you do from this image. Choose the picture well, as it will work hardest to get you gigs and a following. Surfers will only progress into the website and check out your amazing playing and stage performance if they like the look of that first image.

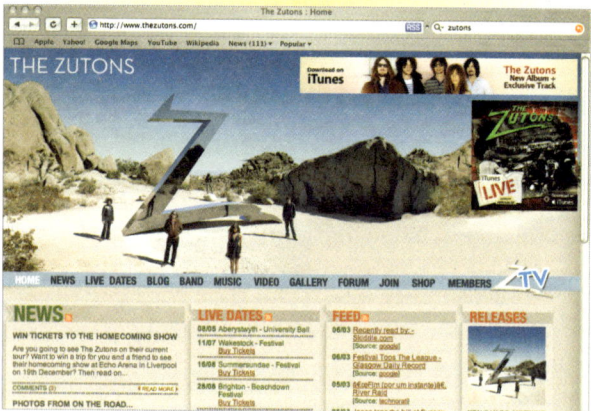

▲ *Choose a striking picture of the band for your home page.*

● ●

▼ *Dark text on a light background is easier to read than vice versa.*

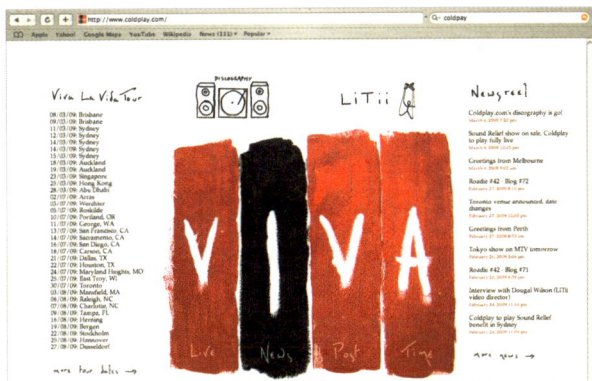

Make sure your website is easy to read. Choose your text and background colours with care. Dark text on a light background is easier to read than the other way round. You also don't want to set your text size too small to be easily read or too large so it appears to shout. Avoid the overuse of capital letters for the same reason.

The most important thing about any website is to have a clear idea of the impression you want to create and make everything work towards that. Confused messages, clashing images and too many gimmicks will leave the surfer wondering what he/she has got themselves into: a calm and well-focused site will retain their interest.

What To Include?

If you really must have an 'arty' introductory page, always have a Skip Intro function for impatient browsers. Make sure you have a good page title – no wasted words like 'Welcome to the website of…', just key words that say what you do.

Get each band member to write their own biography, giving a target number of words or do them yourself and let them complain!

Gig listings are a must. Add links to each venue's website for info on how to get there. It's also worth creating a poster

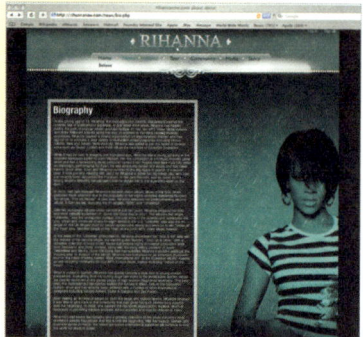

or flyer for each show and making it downloadable so the venue and/or fans can help you publicize the event.

▲ *Fans will be interested in reading your biography.*

▼ *Gig listings are a must!*

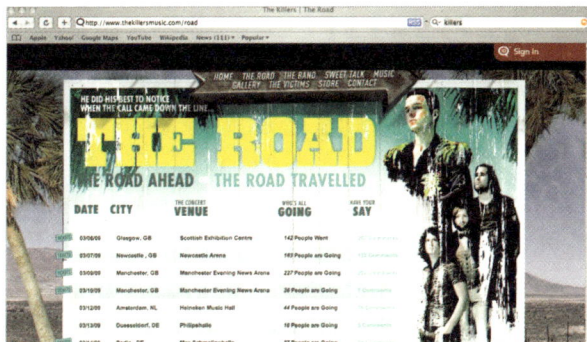

Photos are also a must on websites, either scattered about or in a 'gallery' feature. Encourage fans to send you the pictures and/or videos they take at gigs: seeing them up there will add to the buzz.

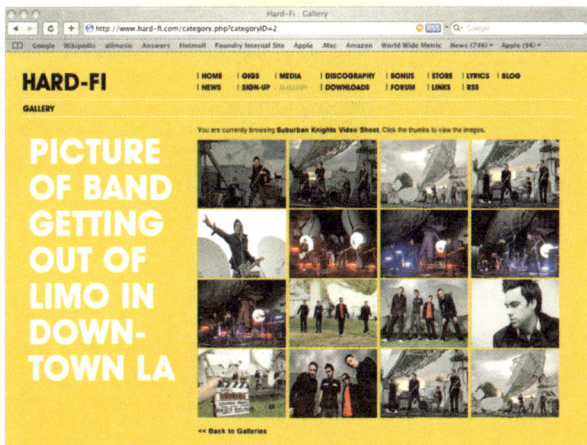

▲ *A photo gallery can create a buzz around your band and your gigs.*

Comments & Messageboards

If you get good comments from venue owners and/or fans, or a great bit of press, put it up on the site. Third-party testimonials, as they're known, carry far more weight than your own claims, so make the most of them.

Having your own messageboard is a great plus, but remember someone will have to moderate it to remove spam attacks, remove abuse or cut out flame wars between fans. Obviously an empty messageboard is a disaster, so make sure that doesn't happen on your site.

Think about having a 'members only' section so your keenest fans feel they have access to something exclusive. Those who want to join them can then be encouraged!

▼ *A good messageboard can help create a buzz, so it's important to give it some care and attention.*

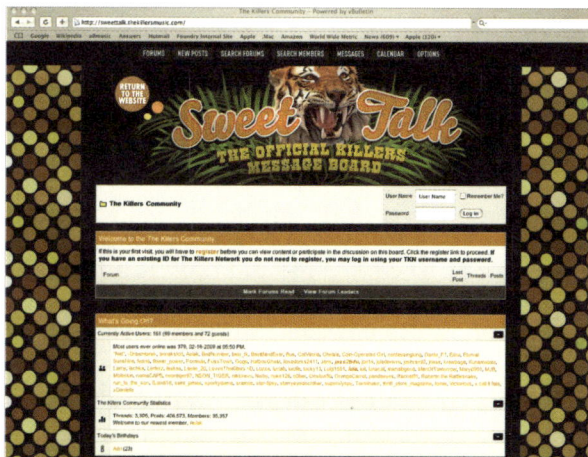

HANDY HINTS

Links from MySpace, gig guides, other bands and agents will increase your Google ranking. That's links from their site to yours. Outbound links linking to their site from yours does nothing for your Google ranking and may hurt you once you start getting a good ranking.

You can add 'alt text' to your images to encourage search engines to pick them up. Don't overdo it, though. One or two key words per image will encourage another way into your site.

Don't forget links to MP3 sites that feature your music. And, last but not least, your contact information should be easy to find: give email addresses and mobile phone numbers, but it's best to avoid putting your landline or physical address on the web.

▲ *Don't forget to include contact information.*

What Software Do You Need?

Once upon a time British rock groups like the Who (ask your parents!) formed at art school. And certainly some artistic ability will help you in getting a website together, but the tools of the job is software. If your aim is to make music, you may be better off subcontracting site-building to a friend who got an A in computer studies: the amount of time this could take up is no laughing matter.

HANDY HINTS

Get your mates involved! You may not be able to pay them now but imagine the acclaim they'll get when you're famous! If you have friends with computer skills, or aspirations of graphic design or photography, enlist their talents to help with your website and content.

▼ *It can take a long time to build a good site.*

For a start, the number of acronyms and confusing terms are enough to put most people off – in which case, settle for a MySpace Music page. Still with us? Okay, the first thing you will need is an image editing programme to help with layout and image content (photos etc). Well-known examples are Photoshop and Paintshop Pro (PC, for web graphics).

Then you will need a page editor. WYSIWYG editor (What You See Is What You Get) is a package that lets you build the website as you see it. Microsoft Word can help create a basic website structure of HTML pages but can be limited. Microsoft FrontPage is available with some versions of Microsoft Office on some PCs. Dreamweaver is a programme specifically for web designers but too specialist for the rest of us. (If you haven't yet brought in a knowledgeable friend to help you, now could be the time!)

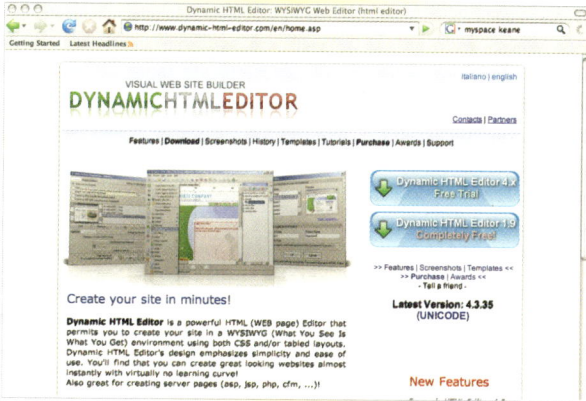

▲ *Download a free WYSIWYG editor from www.dynamic-html-editor.com*

◄ *It may be simplest and easiest to settle for a MySpace page.*

http://www.dynamic-html-editor.com is a free downloadable WYSIWYG editor. The cheapest option to write HTML is Notepad, which comes bundled with all but the most basic PC.

Free FTP software to upload your website from computer to your webspace is available at:

☆ GoFTP (http://www.goftp.com)

☆ FileZilla (http://filezilla-project.org/)

This is usually as simple as dragging files from your desktop window into the 'webspace' window and hitting the 'upload' button.

▲ *Free FTP software to upload your website from your computer to your webspace is available at http://filezilla-project.org*

Getting Webspace

Your best bet for obtaining a free website is to host your information on a MySpace page. Free webspace is harder to come by these days and is usually marred with online advertising banners or pop-ups that will compensate for the lack of 'cyber rent'. But if you are serious and are looking for webspace you will need to purchase it.

The same goes for registering a domain name of your own (like http://www.domainname.co.uk). This gets you an official address for your website on the World Wide Web. This address is how the rest of the world can find you. The reason for the cost is that the central 'address book' of all the world's domain names needs to be updated – which has to be paid for.

▲ *What will your domain name be?*

Don't use free space masquerading as a real website (that's where your url says www.mybandname.co.uk but it's actually located on www.aband.cheapspace .co.uk) Google specifically excludes sites in that situation and will not 'spider' (search) the pages, so nothing except the domain name or url will be visible on Google. If that is a problem, you will have to get real webspace (also known as hosting) from sites such as UK2.net or Easily.co.uk

Practically speaking, there is really no difference these days between the suffices on web addresses, like .com, .co.uk and .net. Search engines don't discriminate

▲ *Get webspace from www.uk2.net*

▼ *Get webspace from http://easily.co.uk*

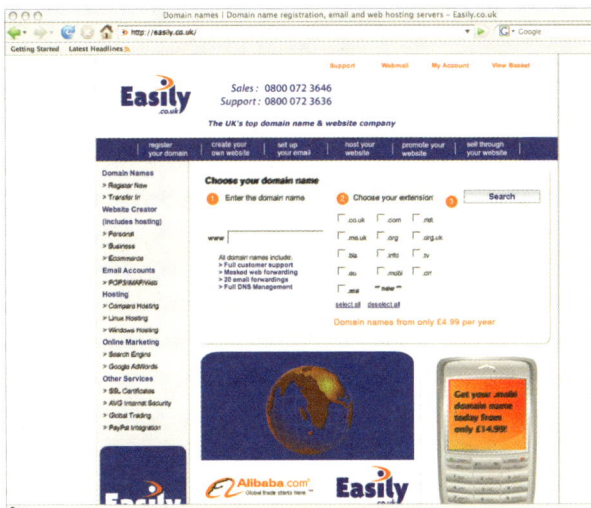

between them, though some people tend to type in .com automatically as it was the first publicly known domain extension. So when registering a domain name, you may wish to go for the .com first and, if it is taken, try for any of the others. (.co.uk, .net, .org, .tv, etc.)

It's worth noting an address is not the same as a domain name of the same name with a different extension. Each of the addresses must be registered separately.

Using HTML

If you have never heard of HTML, this could be the time to call in help! The acronym stands for Hyper Text Markup Language, and it is a text-based text formatting description. Basically you use commands within brackets that look like this <P> and this will determine how the text that follows looks on the completed site. The commands will be invisible to the user.

HTML has been around a long time, and like anything old has certain drawbacks. These include:

☆ You can't control the precise layout; each web client will display your page in a slightly different way.

☆ You cannot centre images or text; everything is left-justified.

☆ You cannot include tables or mathematical symbols in your text – unlikely for a music site anyway.

Many people feel you needn't bother learning HTML as automatic converters exist that will do the job for you.

HANDY HINTS

There are HTML generators online where you can put in your keywords/description etc. and it will put together the HTML text for you!

Others believe HTML will give you far better control over the process and ultimately your websites. You will have a far deeper understanding of the web, and as a result you will create better websites more quickly. (Only useful if and when you want to repeat the process!) There are books and online tutorials that will teach you, should you wish to go that way.

▲ *The HTML commands will be invisible to the user.*

Try these online HTML tutorials:

☆ http://www.webdevelopersnotes.com/
tutorials/html/

☆ http://www.myhtmltutorials.com/

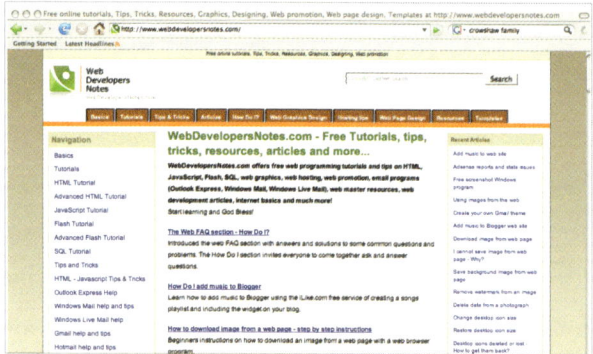

▲ *www.webdevelopersnotes.com has lots of information to help you build a website.*

▲ *www.myhtmltutorials.com does what it says on the tin!*

Basic Website Design

What is the difference between a web page and a website? A website is a group of web pages connected together through links. HTML has a special tag called the 'link' tag that does this vital job.

Website templates can be very useful; they can be used to 'jump-start' the creation of a website. They are also a way for people to put out great-looking websites quickly with little or no knowledge of HTML and web design. And let's face it, a great-looking website is what we're in this for.

HANDY HINTS

Google 'website templates' and you'll find load of free ready-made shells you can copy and use as the basis of your site.

All navigational buttons and tabs should be clearly labelled and easy to read. It is more important that they are easy to read and understand than be good-looking. It's also important visitors should be able to find what they're looking for within three clicks. If not, they are likely to click off your site as quickly as they clicked on.

User-friendliness is all-important. Check how long it takes for your pages to download. Studies have shown that most visitors will lose interest in your site if the majority of a page does not download within 15 seconds. Clever ideas like animation should therefore be avoided if their use increases download time.

▲ *Navigational buttons and tabs should be clearly labelled and easy to read.*

▼ *Styling should be consistent throughout the site.*

Just as with a magazine or book, styles used should be consistent throughout the site. Colours, backgrounds, textures and special effects should be looked at very carefully. The best rule of thumb is to keep it simple – if in doubt, throw it out.

HANDY HINTS

Keep the alignment of your main website text to the left, not centred, so your visitors will be comfortable with what they are reading. Centred text is best left for headlines.

FTP

Once designed, you transfer your website to your host's server using an FTP (File Transfer Protocol) programme. There are several free programmes you can use to move your files and many HTML editors and web design programmes like Dreamweaver have FTP capabilities built in. Another option is Internet Explorer, whose version 5 and upwards has an FTP programme built in.

If you're looking for a book to guide you, Amazon do a list of all-time best web design books you can choose from:

☆ http://www.amazon.com/All-Time-Best-Design-related-Books/lm/2NEA2A89WNOE2

As well as books, there are many good web resources that will help you get a site. Here are a selection:

☆ http://www.grantasticdesigns.com/5rules.html

☆ http://www.webdesign.org/web/web-design-
   basics/design-principles/basic-rules-on-web-
   design.4316.html

☆ http://www.dazines.co.uk/articles/2009/feb/the-
   basic-web-design-rules.php

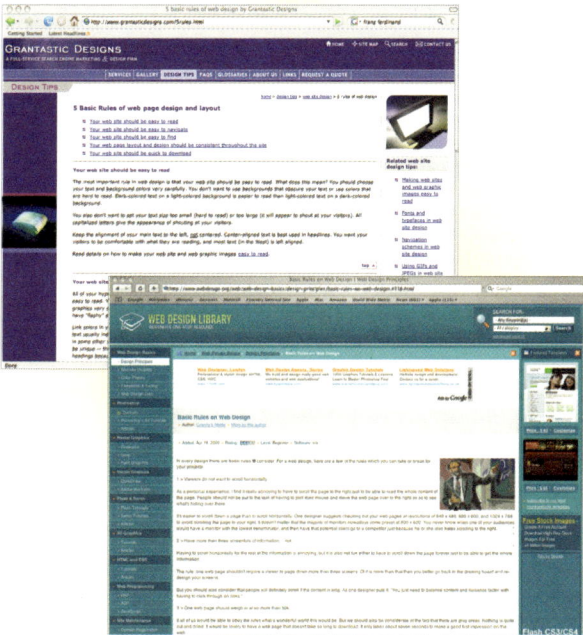

▲ *There are many good web resources that will help you create a
site, such as www.grantasticdesigns.com and www.webdesign.org*

Summary

Check your progress against this list

Write down the aims of your site before
you lift a finger and make sure what you
create reflects these . . . . □

Consider using a website template for
your first attempt – most people will not
notice the difference . . . . □

Use the best image you have of the
band or singer on the home page . . . . □

Make sure text is the right size and colour
to be legible; avoid background clutter . . . . □

Don't get hung up on HTML . . . . □

Don't be too mean to buy webspace . . . . □

Buy the best domain name (band-name address)
possible – and make it .com for preference . . . . □

If all this is too much for now, at least
get on MySpace! . . . . □

1

2

3

4

5

6

7

8

9

10

11

12

PROMOTING YOUR WEBSITE

Introduction

So you've got your own website – now you need to tell the world it's there! Of course you can do the obvious things like include it in the signature of every email you send and write it large on your social networking profile page, but there are many tricks of the trade it's worth learning that will put you one important step ahead of the pack.

1
2
3
4
5
6
7
8
9
10
11
12

Creating An Online Fan Network

If you want to build a following, you need to turn passive fans into an active 'street team' pushing your music. Encourage them to tell people what a great time they had at your gig – via your MySpace comments section, YouTube films and comments, chat rooms, forums, review sites, Facebook – basically anywhere your prospective future fans, management, booker or record label could be reading.

Ask people to write reviews of your music, then post them on your site. They'll be as thrilled to see their work and name in print as you will be to get praise! The same goes with pictures. Sometimes all a new potential fan needs is a

▼ *Get your fans to comment on your MySpace page.*

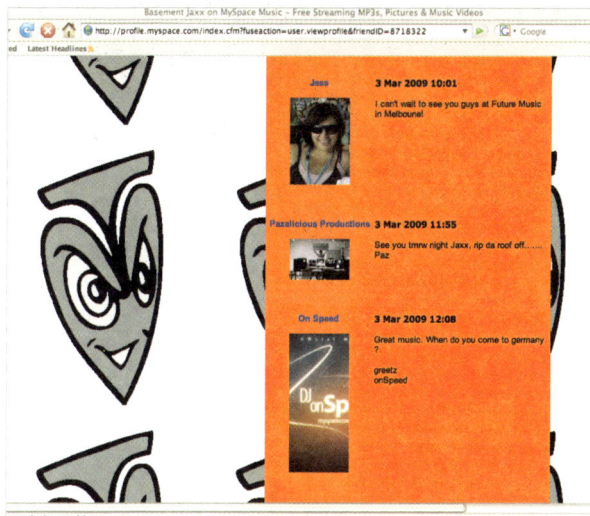

little confirmation that other people enjoy your music as well, so it's great to have kindred spirits reinforcing the 'brand'!

HANDY HINTS

Use sites like YouTube to mention your site through comments to your clips.

◄ *Get fans to write about what a great time they had at your gig online.*

Add forums or messageboards to your site where your fans can communicate and keep them returning (more details may be found elsewhere). If fans feel like they have friends on your site they will feel an even stronger connection to your music.

▲ *A messageboard or forum enables fans to communicate and may encourage them to keep returning.*

Street Teams & Fans

Some 'street teams' visit gigs, clubs and shops giving out stickers, leaflets and promo items. But even if you don't want to get that formal, nominating a 'fan of the month' costs nothing and will make your followers feel their efforts are valued. Another way to encourage your fans to spread the word is by giving them access to exclusive video footage or audio of forthcoming releases before anyone else sees or hears it. But you need to do this without making anyone feel excluded.

HANDY HINTS

Active fans are 10 times as much use in promoting your act and the site than passive 'lurkers' – so keep them onside at all times. Reward them with the occasional badge or sticker every so often for their help.

HANDY HINTS

Sign up to cafepress.co.uk and upload band artwork to produce t-shirts, mugs, tote bags and more, all displayed in your own online shop, and link these to your webspace or MySpace page for fans to order. Make sure they all have your web address on!

Last but not least, linking with other bands after you have played gigs together may well turn their fans into yours. The music business is competitive, for sure, but in the cyber world the more friends you have the better.

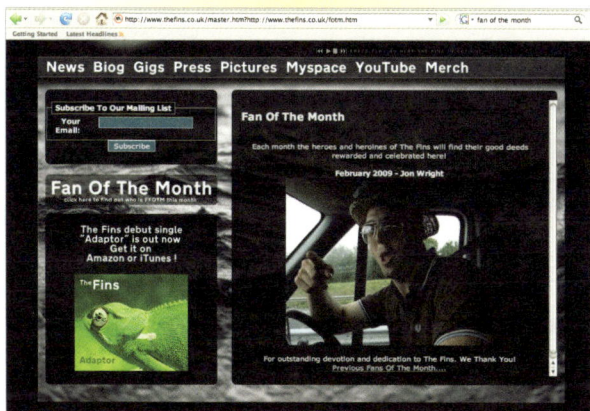

▲ *Having a 'Fan of the Month' makes your followers feel valued.*

Targeting Fan Sites & E-zines

E-zines (a contraction of the words 'electronic magazine') are publications distributed by email or posted on a website for readers to access via the web. They are typically tightly focused on a subject area. They are similar to online magazines, which may also be published as physical magazines and be variations thereof (for example www.nme.com and www.q4music.com). They will try and make their money through online advertising to make up for the loss of a cover price.

▼ *Identify e-zines that deal with the type of music you create: e.g. www.punkupdates.com, which reviews and discusses punk music.*

You need to identify the e-zines that deal with the kind of music you create. Then you need to get them writing about you. The approach can either come from yourselves or, if you organize them, your fans.

◄ *Some online magazines, such as www.nme.com, are also published as physical magazines.*

Perhaps the best place to find your targets are websites like the E-zine Directory (http://www.ezine-dir.com/). But better still is to check the websites of the bands you align yourself with and see who has been writing about them in their reviews section. Then search out these e-zines and put them on your mailing list. Approach any writer you think may be sympathetic and make sure they are supplied with new music as it is recorded. Follow up with an email politely asking what they thought. Make them feel you value their opinion highly.

▼ *Search for fan sites at www.fan-sites.org*

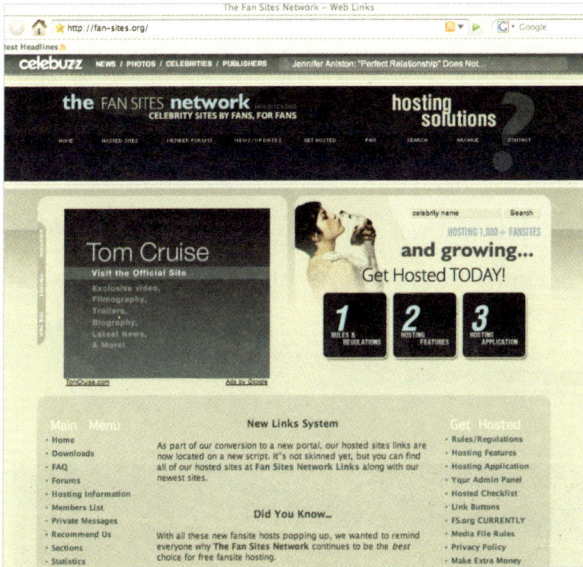

Fan sites exist for all kinds of music and fashion: try a guide like http://www.fan-sites.org/, but be prepared for plenty of dead links. These sites tend to have a limited life, so ask around to find out which are 'happening' at the moment.

◄ *Search for e-zines to target at www.ezine-dir.com*

Using Mailing Lists

Mailing lists are a great way for visitors who regularly visit your website to get up-to-date news straight to their inbox. It saves them fruitlessly checking back if nothing has happened – all the more reason to freshen up your site at least twice a week!

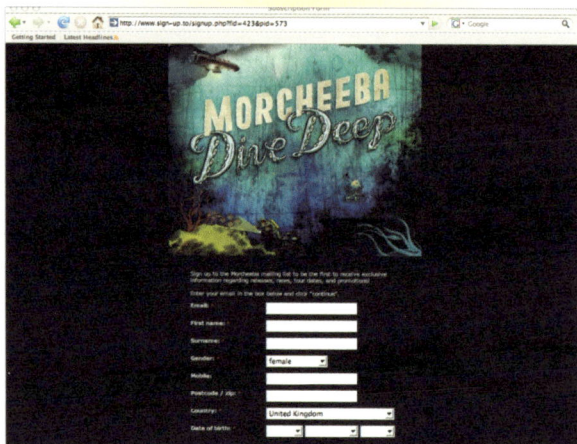

▲ *Mailing lists are a great way to update your fans of your movements straight to their inboxes.*

▼ *Everyone who has seen you at a gig is a potential member of your mailing list.*

Everyone who has seen you at a gig is a potential member of your mailing list, so don't let them leave before they have given you their email addresses. Have a clipboard and pen handy to let them write them down – you could even offer them an incentive from the stage and say that anyone who signs up at half time will be in a draw for a free sampler CD.

▲ *Offer your fans an incentive to join your mailing list so that you can update them regularly.*

▼ *There are a number of websites you can use to help set up a mailing list such as http://notifylist.com*

A 'notify list' is particularly useful. It is a one-way mailing list you can use to let your website's visitors know every time you update your site with new features, news, live dates, etc.

There are a number of websites you can use to help you set up a list. Most offer the service free. Adding a new mailing list to your site can be done in less than five minutes with very little computer knowledge required. Simply create an account, fill in the mailing list details and put a small, relevant piece of code on to the site to allow people to subscribe.

Here are a few that may help:

☆ http://www.aardvarkmailinglist.net/

☆ http://notifylist.com/

☆ http://www.yourmailinglistprovider.com/

☆ http://www.freelists.org/

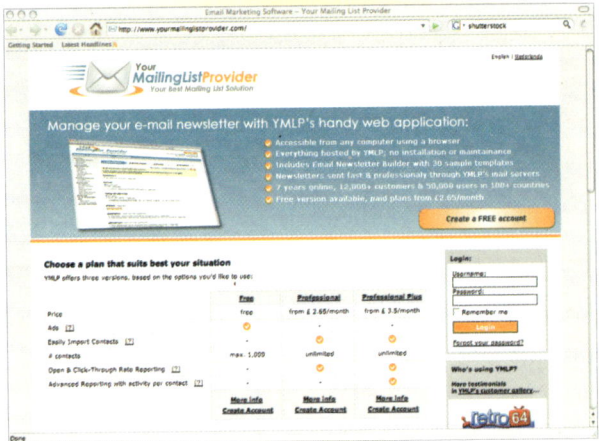

▲ *Adding a mailing list to your site is quick and easy. Try using www.yourmailinglistprovider.com*

Using Messageboards

Fans love messageboards because it gives them the chance to make their point and interact with each other. At its lowest level it is like the wall of the school toilet – and remarks can be just as gross – but if run correctly people participating in an Internet forum can form bonds with one another and, most importantly, your music.

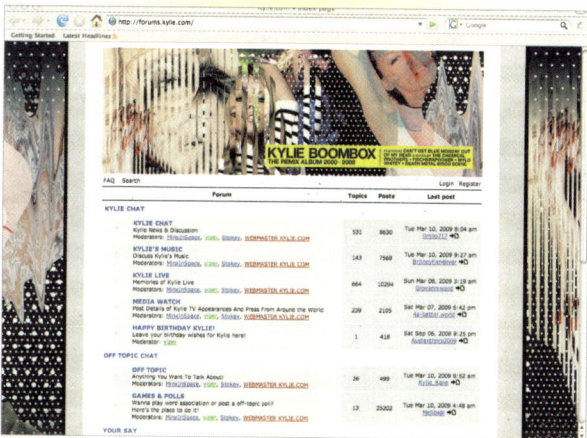

▲ *Fans love forums and messageboards as it gives them the chance to make their point and interact.*

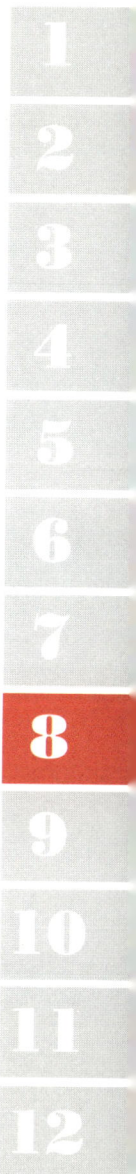

Most Internet forums require registration to post. Registered users of the site are referred to as members and are allowed to submit or send electronic messages. A set of elite individuals, commonly referred to as administrators and moderators, will keep the forums governed smoothly.

It is a good idea to create a FAQ (Frequently Asked Questions) section containing basic information for new members and people not yet familiar with the use and principles of forums in general, and yours in particular.

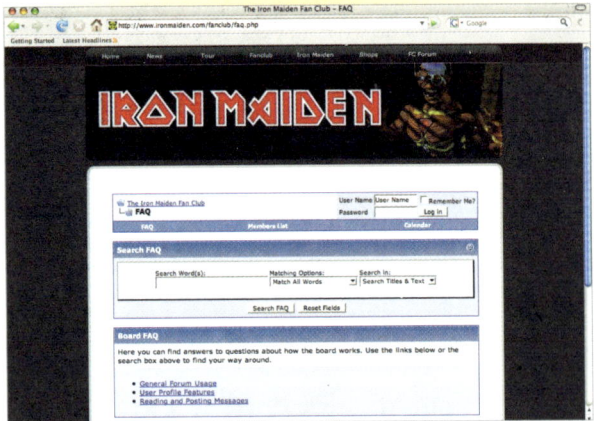

▲ *It is a good idea to create a FAQ section for your forum.*

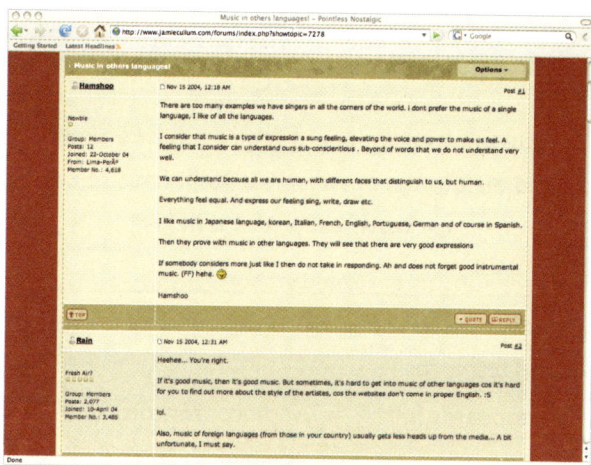

A thread is a collection of posts, displayed from oldest to latest. Each thread will have a title, decided on by the original poster (OP for short) who began the dialogue or made the announcement. A thread can contain any number of posts, including multiple posts from the same members, even if they are one after the other. An 'ignore' function allows members to hide posts of other members that they do not want to see or have a problem with.

▲ *A thread is a collection of posts, displayed from oldest to latest.*

HANDY HINTS

If your messageboard is quiet, start a topic to encourage posters. You don't have to be controversial ... but it helps!

Useful resources:

☆ Proboards (http://www.proboards.com/)

☆ vBulletin (http://www.vbulletin.com/)

▲ *You can create your own forum for free at www.proboards.com*

Using Meta-tagging

Meta-tagging is a way of getting ahead of your 'rival' sites and coming as high as you can in the Internet search engines by using keywords. It was originally intended to help search engines categorize sites correctly when introduced in the mid- to late 1990s, but webmasters quickly learned the significance of having the right meta element, as it frequently led to a high ranking in the search engines and, through this, generated increased traffic to the website.

▲ Meta-tagging is a way of ensuring that your site comes as high as possible in an Internet search engine by using keywords.

263

▼ *A high ranking generates increased traffic to your site and more exposure for your band.*

Meta elements provide information about a given web page. They are inserted into the HTML document, but are not directly visible to a user visiting the site. Some search engines read the content of the tag and reference the words within it along with the page's regular body copy, so you can have two bites at the cherry.

At the end of the day, your page/site's title and description are what attract the interest of the user. They should also aptly describe the content of your site. If you want to use a 'keyword' meta-tag to list key words for the document, use a list of words that relate to each specific page on your site instead of using one broad set of keywords for every page. Site owners who concentrate on creating good meta-tags for their pages have consistently found it can help with ranking across all major search engine 'web crawlers'.

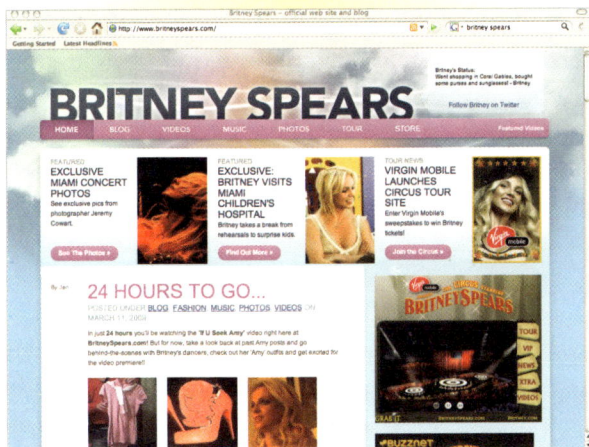

▲ *Your site's title and description are what attract the interest of the user.*

Google Site Indexing

Google says it does not use HTML or meta-tag elements for indexing. The Director of Research at Google, Monika Henziger, was quoted in 2002 as saying, 'Currently we don't trust meta-data because we are afraid of being manipulated.' Other search engines developed techniques to penalize websites considered to be 'cheating' the system. For example, a site repeating the same meta keyword several times may have its ranking decreased. In practice, a search engine will probably ignore the meta keyword element completely, regardless of how many words are used in the element.

Google does, however, use meta-tag elements for displaying site links. The title tags are used to create the link in search results.

▶ *www.onlinemetatag.com is a meta-tag generator.*

There are meta-tag generators available into which you input your information, which then generates the HTML to place the 'head' tags in your website. One of these is http://www.onlinemetatag.com/

HANDY HINTS

Google offers a 'Dissatisfied? Help Us Improve' link at the bottom of the results page when you search for something. This leads to a form where you can enter the URL you were looking for – thus letting you enter the URL of your site!

Summary

Check your progress against this list

Promoting a website is a never-ending obligation!
Points to remember:

Don't let it get obviously out-of-date . . . . ☐

Make your fans feel like they belong
by enlisting them in your 'street team' . . . . ☐

Keep a list of relevant fansites and e-zines
and develop a relationship with them . . . . ☐

Keep your fans coming back via
the 'notify list' function . . . . ☐

Don't forget to freshen up your site
at least twice a week . . . . ☐

Get a messageboard attached to your site . . . . ☐

Use meta-tags but be aware these are
not as important as most people think . . . . ☐

DISTRIBUTING YOUR MUSIC ONLINE

Introduction

The formats in which music has been marketed – the transition from vinyl and cassette through compact disc to MP3 file – has been mirrored by the means of distributing it to the people who want to hear it: your audience. Yet while physical formats survive, for sale through online shops or merchandise at gigs, it makes sense to trade in both markets. This section points out the pros and the pitfalls of distributing your music online, the help you'll need and where you might find it.

1
2
3
4
5
6
7
8
9
10
11
12

Uploading Tracks To The Web

You will probably store your music as MP3 files. The reason these are so popular is that they are audio files compressed to save space while still giving reasonable sound quality. They are ideal to upload to the Internet but how you do this will depend on where you wish to put them.

The simplest way is to use a site like http://www.putfile .com, which allows you to post your music and let others access it, much as you would holiday snaps.If you want

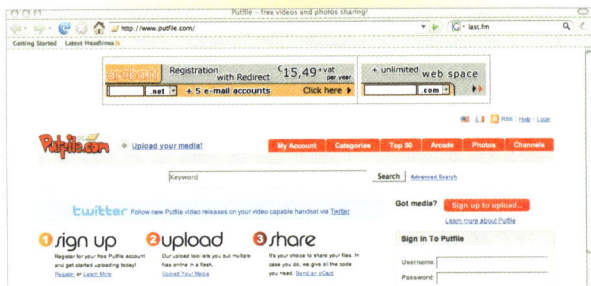

▲ *www.putfile.com allows you to post your music and let others access it for free.*

▼ *www.last.fm has widgets that enable you to upload music to your social networking page.*

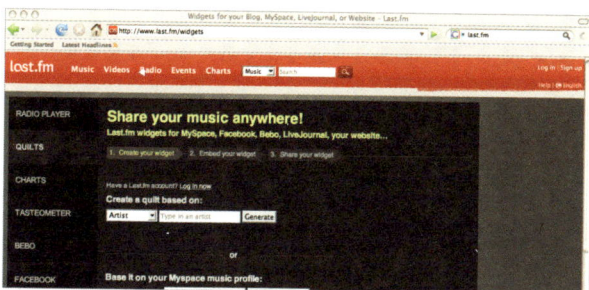

to upload your music to your social networking page, they will supply a widget to allow that to happen. If you post your music to a jukebox or radio service like last.fm, you will be able to manage your presence through their Music Manager software. It's free to register, add music and to use all of the main features of the last.fm label site. They do offer some advanced promotional features; however these are purely optional, and cost a minimal amount should you wish to use them.

HANDY HINTS

Don't upload whole songs to your social networking sites; just give 30-second 'tasters' to leave them wanting more.

Music Download Sales & Bandwidth

There are programmes available like Website Music Player that claim to let you sell your music online (via MySpace and Facebook) to anyone with a credit card or PayPal account. After successful payment, the customer is forwarded to a download page that contains only the songs that they've paid for. The customer is only allowed to download each song a set number of times (determined by you in your settings), after which the download links expire and delete themselves to prevent them from being shared.

If you pay for your own webspace, ensure there is enough room to upload music files. This is where sites such as MySpace and other streaming sites really help as listening to music files hosted on your own webspace eats up 'bandwidth'. If your site is popular and all your bandwidth is used up, your site can

▼ *Programmes like Website Music Player let you sell your music online. Download from www.websitemusicplayer.com*

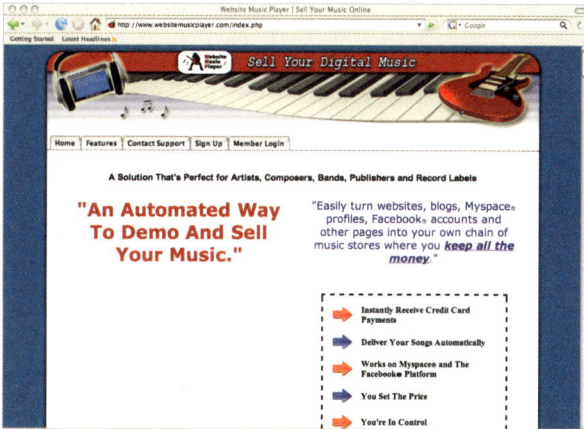

temporarily shut down. It might be beneficial to link to your MySpace page, PureVolume page and/or YouTube pages to watch/listen to videos and audio and keep your website for words and pictures.

HANDY HINTS

Uploading originals rather than cover versions to MySpace may avoid copyright hassles.

File-sharing

A peer-to-peer (or P2P) computer network uses connectivity between participants in a network and the cumulative bandwidth of network participants rather than a conventional centralized server or servers. A pure P2P network does not have clients or servers, as such, but only equal peer nodes that simultaneously function as both 'clients' and 'servers' to the other nodes on the network.

The advantage here is that files can be shared without having access to a proper server, and because of this there is little accountability for the contents of the files. Hence, these networks tend to be very popular for illicit files such as music, movies, pirated software, etc.

▶ *Peer-to-peer (or P2P) is another way of file-sharing.*

▼ *Files can be shared without having access to a proper server.*

The Usenet binary newsgroups is another method of file distribution, one that is substantially different from other methods. Files transferred over Usenet are often subject to miniscule windows of opportunity. Typical retention time of binary news servers are often as low as 24 hours, and having a posted file available for a week is considered a long time. However, the Usenet model is relatively efficient, in that the messages are passed around a large web of peers from one news server to another, and finally fanned out to the end user from there.

▼ *You should regard P2P file-sharing as a promotional tool, not as a way of making money.*

You can use this to distribute your music, though in terms of being paid for the privilege you should regard it as a promotional tool. See Google BitTorrent for more information.

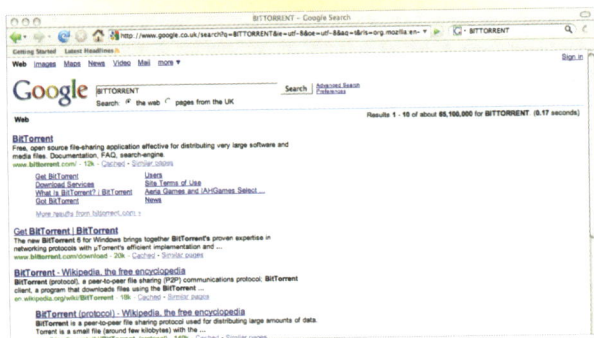

▲ *See Google 'BitTorrent' for more information.*

Using MP3 Sites

PureVolume.com and Unsigned.com are sites for finding out about new bands, making them ideal for unknown bands that want to promote themselves.

PureVolume is a website for the discovery and promotion of new music and emerging artists. Each artist has a profile that typically contains basic info, updates, photos, shows and music for streaming.

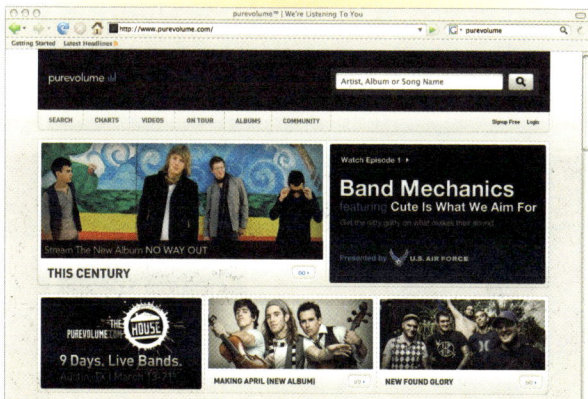

▲ *You can host MP3s, make friends with other artists and promote gigs on www.purevolume.com*

▼ *An artist profile on www.purevolume.com – this could be you!*

Artists have the option of making each of their songs available for free download. Listeners and fans can also create profiles to interact with artists and each other, as well as track and share music they like.

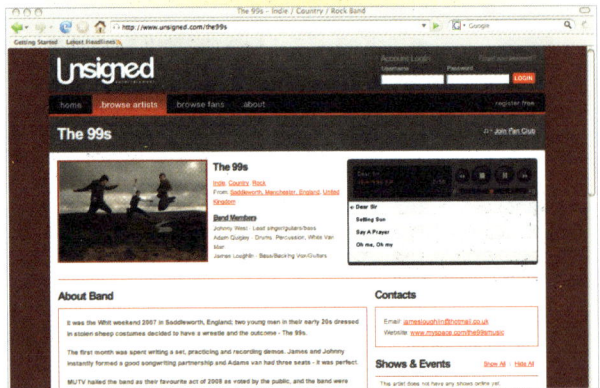

▼ *It is free to create an artist account on www.unsigned.com where people can find out about you and listen to your music.*

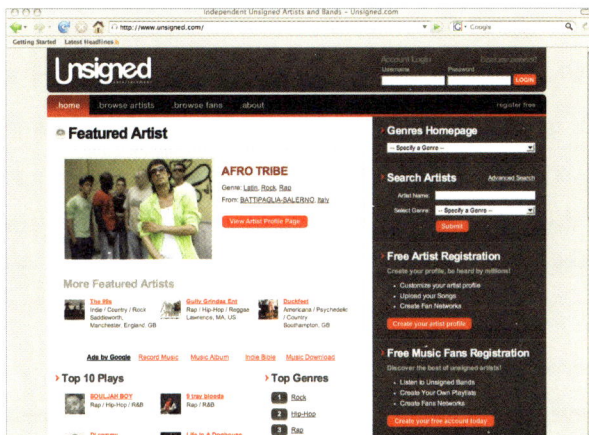

Unsigned.com is a website for unsigned artists and bands to host their MP3s and get exposure. Based in the States, it allows you to browse artists by country. At the time of writing 154 British acts had signed up, with styles ranging from indie through hip hop to hardcore. You create an artist account, which is free, and people can find out about you and listen to your music.

◄ *www.unsigned.com is a website for unsigned artists and bands to host their MP3s and get exposure.*

Podcasting

A blog (or weblog, as they were originally known) is a great way to keep your fans in touch with your activities and make them feel a part of your life – or at least an interested onlooker! Lily Allen used the tactic very astutely, and you can too.

A Podcast is basically an audio blog, and is arguably even more intimate. Not only do they get the inside track, it comes from the horse's mouth! But how do you do it, and what's the score about uploading it to your website? Here are a few hints.

The first is to write a script. You may think you can do it all off the top of your head, but it's well worth having some bullet points so you remember your train of thought – and a stopwatch to avoid going on too long! If you plan to use your own music, there will presumably be no copyright issues, but again be clear in your intentions and have someone else cue the music as required.

You then need to set up your recording equipment. You'll need a computer with a soundcard. You'll also need a microphone – maybe a headset mic, or a basic uni-directional dynamic mic with a suitable connector for your soundcard (a 3.5 mm jack, not an XLR connector).

You then need some audio recording software to allow you to record, edit and tidy your podcast. Your PC's soundcard may have come bundled with software, but if not there's WebPodStudio, PodProducer, Audacity and the professional-quality Adobe Audition.

Promoting Podcasts

Use your existing website to promote your podcast. Upload the MP3 file, then find a way of directing users to click on the link. You could also create an RSS feed of your podcast using programmes like Feedforall, ListGarden or Podifier to create an XML file that

▲ *All you need to record your podcast is a computer with a soundcard, a microphone and some audio recording software.*

contains details of your Podcast. Then simply upload the XML file to your website. You could also submit your podcast RSS feed to some of the major podcast directories like www.podcastingnews.com, www.podcast pickle.com, www.podcastdirectory.com or iTunes, which also has a large podcast directory. To submit a feed to iTunes, you need to create an iTunes account. Although submission is free, you have to enter your credit card details to allow verification of your identity.

YouTube has an online tutorial:

☆ http://www.youtube.com/watch?v=-hrBbczS9Io

▲ *iTunes has a large podcast directory.*

The Distribution Channels

Distributors work with independent labels to distribute products to record shops and the public. But record shops are closing – Woolworths and Zavvi the latest in 2008 – and the problems the world economy is currently experiencing, along with the rise of digital music as the industry standard, means that the physical CD's days are numbered. The overheads involved in manufacturing, shipping, returns and fees make it almost impossible for an independent label or the artists on that label to make any real money from physical CD sales.

▲ *It's difficult to make much money from the sale of physical CDs.*

HANDY HINTS

Work out the production cost of physical CDs and see if working with a distributor is viable. Otherwise save them for sale at gigs where you receive 100 per cent of income.

Yet the likes of Amazon, Play and CD Baby still deal in physical CDs, while HMV combines physical shops with an online presence. So the CD isn't quite dead yet.

▲ *The CD isn't dead yet!*

▼ *CD Baby is an online record store that sells albums by independent musicians.*

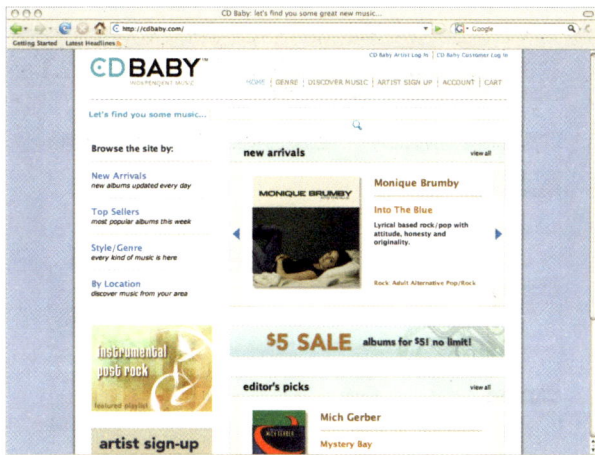

A distributor is a company that will sell your CD in exchange for a set fee. You agree a deal with the distributor, they hold your CD in stock in their warehouse and ship them to shops or Internet site warehouses as demand dictates. Three months later you will receive a percentage of the CD selling price. You, hopefully, have done your sums and the money you receive will exceed the cost of producing the CD in the first place. (Note that if your CD doesn't sell fast enough you may be charged warehouse storage fees.)

▼ *HMV combines physical shops with an online presence.*

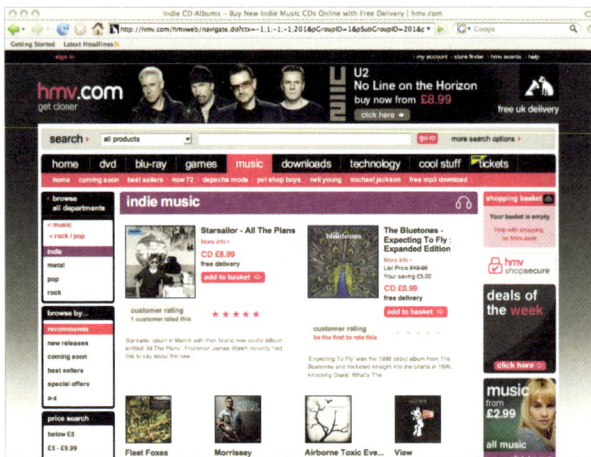

Some of these companies also offer value-added services including credit card terminals to carry to shows, placement on music services such as iTunes and MusicMatch and promotional items and publicity.

HANDY HINTS

Investigate distributors' websites and, if you can, contact their client bands to ask if they are happy with the service they are given.

Targeting National Distributors

A good distributor will not charge you more than a small set-up fee to get started. A nominal fee is common to help defray the costs of stocking your CD, but paying for more than that isn't usual. You can still turn a profit despite paying this fee if you promote your release well.

HANDY HINTS

When you're looking for a distributor, check with bands you know on who they use; you might be surprised at what you find out.

Pinnacle, the UK's biggest independent distributor, closed its doors in 2008, but there are still distributors of 'independent music' to be found. We list some websites overleaf:

☆ **Absolute** – http://www.absolutemarketing.co.uk/

☆ **ADA** – http://www.ada-music.com/faq.php

☆ **Cadiz** – http://www.cadizmusic.co.uk/intro.htm

☆ **Cargo** – http://www.cargorecords.co.uk/contact

☆ **Essential** – http://www.essential-music.com/distribution.html

☆ **Kudos Records** – http://www.kudosrecords.co.uk/index.php?page=info

☆ **PIAS UK** (previously VITAL) – http://www.pias.com/uk/

☆ **Plastichead** – http://www.plastichead.com/about.asp

☆ **Proper** – http://www.properdistribution.com/index.php

☆ **Republic of Music** – http://www.republicofmusic.net/#/about/

☆ **Right Track Distribution** – http://www.righttrackdistribution.co.uk/index.html

☆ **RSK** – http://www.rskentertainment.co.uk/

☆ **Shellshock** – http://www.shellshock.co.uk/contacts.php

☆ **SRD** (Southern Record Distributors) – http://www.srd.co.uk/

▼ *Founded in 1993, ADA is the largest distributor of physical and digital independent music in America.*

▲ *New on the scene, Republic of Music was founded in 2007.*

Summary

Check your progress against this list

Decide if you are looking for exposure
or profit – i.e. a small number of tracks
to create a buzz or whole albums for money . . . . ☐

Upload music to your social networking
sites to give fans a taster of what you do . . . . ☐

Look at the potential of MP3 sites
to sell your product . . . . ☐

Peer-to-peer (P2P) file-sharing is regarded
as 'shady' due to lack of regulation:
investigate and decide if it's for you . . . . ☐

1
2
3
4
5
6
7
8
9
10
11
12

THE SUCCESS STORIES

Introduction

The Internet may still be in its infancy, but there have already been a number of trailblazing bands that have pushed the envelope and become household names on the basis of their online activities. Fame could have come anyway, of course, but there seems little doubt that their guerrilla tactics in cyberspace hastened the end result. There have also been those who have homed in on their core support once their 15 minutes in the spotlight had faded, and the group that made headlines for 'giving their music away', Radiohead.

1

2

3

4

5

6

7

8

9

10

11

12

Arctic Monkeys

Sheffield-born band the Arctic Monkeys were megastars before they even released their first fully marketed single in October 2005. The group has already built a devoted following by being one of the first to harness the power of the Internet. It all began when demand for their home-recorded CDs exceeded supply at gigs. They gave their blessing to fans copying and distributing their music, and their following mushroomed as tracks were swapped in an example of viral marketing on the Internet.

According to one estimate there were already 142 different versions of various Arctic Monkeys songs floating around on the Internet by the time of their first official release, some of these having been recorded by fans at concerts. Additionally the Monkeys used the net to communicate with their followers on their forum and post tracks and lyrics.

▼ *'I Bet You Look Good On The Dancefloor' debuted at No. 1 on the UK singles chart in October 2005.*

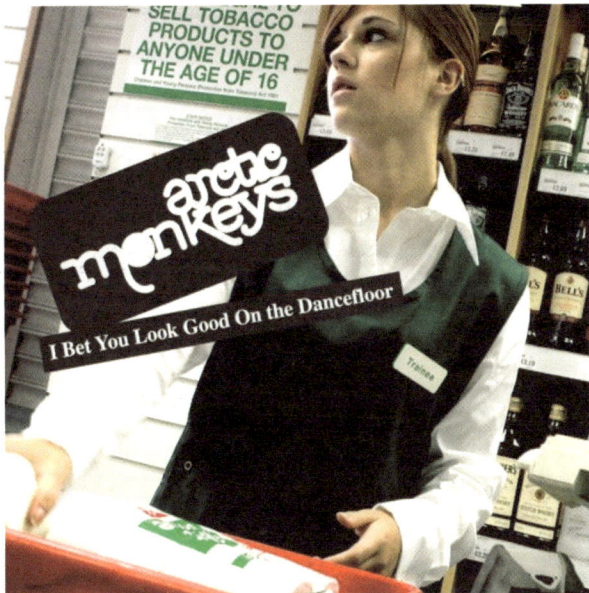

Visits to www.arcticmonkeys.com came from chat rooms and blogs, but search engines became a more important source of visits as the band's reputation grew. When they played their first major London gig to 2,000 fans at the Astoria, the audience sang along to every word of the single, 'I Bet You Look Good On The Dancefloor', which had yet to be released.

▼ *The Arctic Monkeys' website includes news, gig listings, a blog and a forum – all the components of a successful website.*

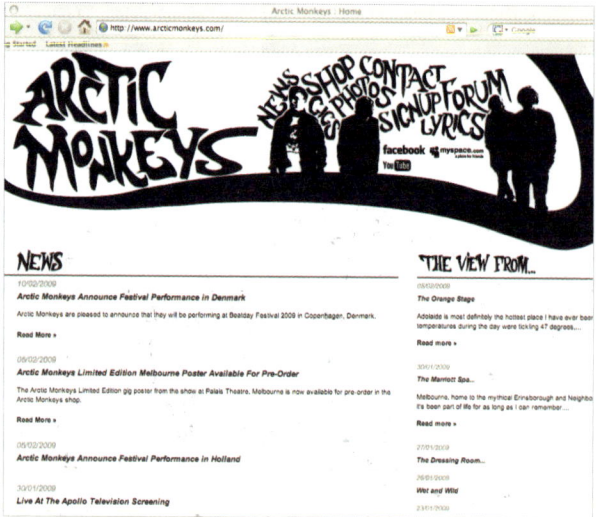

By January 2006, the Arctic Monkeys were the most searched-for band on the Internet, their website the most visited in the Bands and Artists category.

Ironically by the time the Monkeys' second album *Favourite Worst Nightmare* was due for release in April 2007, the record company to which they were signed were so worried about unauthorized leaks that might harm album sales that music writers were not sent advance copies as usual: instead they had to turn up to Arctic Monkeys' London HQ to be played the disc in a room. Mobile phones and tape recorders were presumably left at the door.

▲ *The Arctic Monkeys' debut album* Whatever People Say I Am, That's What I'm Not *was the fastest-selling debut album in British history.*

▼ Favourite Worst Nightmare *was nominated for the 2007 Mercury Prize and won Best British Album at the 2008 BRIT Awards.*

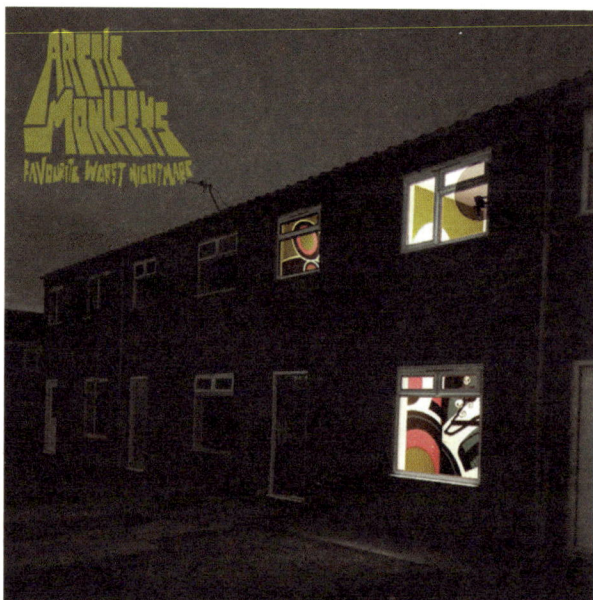

HANDY HINTS

Get a blog going that keeps people abreast of your latest project. And don't forget to update it regularly.

Marillion

British progressive rockers Marillion were first active in the early 1980s, but after a decade in the spotlight it seemed their time had passed. They had other ideas, however, and knew their hardcore of support would be the basis to help them continue making music.

▲ *Marillion were first active in the early 1980s.*

In 1993, some of those fans suggested opening a bank account and donating to allow the band to tour America (with donors still having to buy tickets to shows). From there, the band grew their mailing list to more than 20,000 fans and in 1999, when they released their final album for a record label, decided to use it to fund new albums and release them through their website, www.marillion.com.

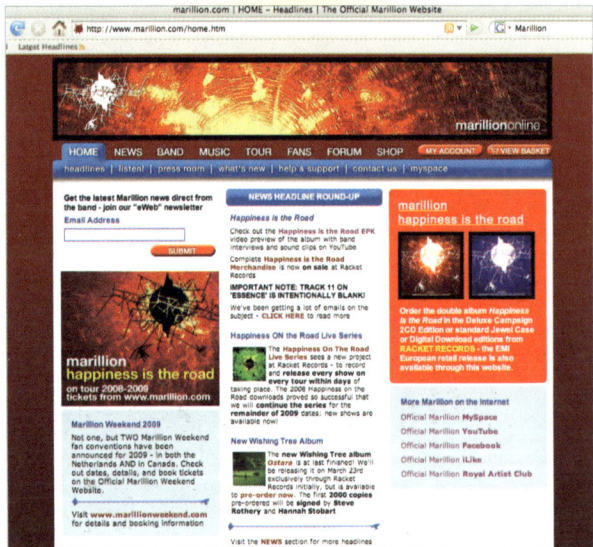

▲ *Marillion have developed one of the most devoted and interactive fan bases in the world.*

▶ *Marillion turned to their fans to finance the making of* Anoraknophobia, *asking them to pre-order the 2001 album before it was even recorded. This was an unprecedented success, with more than 12,500 fans pre-ordering it.*

Marillion released three albums between 2001 and 2007, bucking the decline in CD sales by continuing to build a database of email addresses in excess of 65,000, and offering special edition pre-order CDs with 128-page hardcover books. Hardcore fans were willing to pay £25 or more for these special editions.

HANDY HINTS

If you are asking for donations to complete a project, keep a 'thermometer' on your website of where you've reached. And always fulfil your promise, or refund the donations.

▼ Marbles *was released in 2004. The fans who had pre-ordered it received an exclusive 2-CD version with a booklet containing the names of everyone who had pre-ordered.*

marillion marbles

Their 2008 album, *Happiness Is The Road*, was a double CD offered not only as a download but a physical CD with two hardcover books for the pre-order version. With CD sales at an all-time low, they decided to sell exclusively from their own website. 'This decision was made to drive more traffic to our website, growing our database, and also because ... once everyone in the supply chain has had their cut, there isn't much left for the artist.' Their new single was made available for free download, and fans were invited to create a video and post it to YouTube. The one with the most views by a certain date won a £5,000 cash prize.

▲ *Marillion made 2008's* Happiness Is The Road *free to download from P2P websites.*

Radiohead

Unconventional Brit-rockers Radiohead made history in 2008 by releasing their seventh studio album via their website, potentially for free. Titled *In Rainbows* and unveiled in October, it was the Oxford band's first release after the end of their long-running contract with EMI, and customers could download it for whatever price they saw fit to pay.

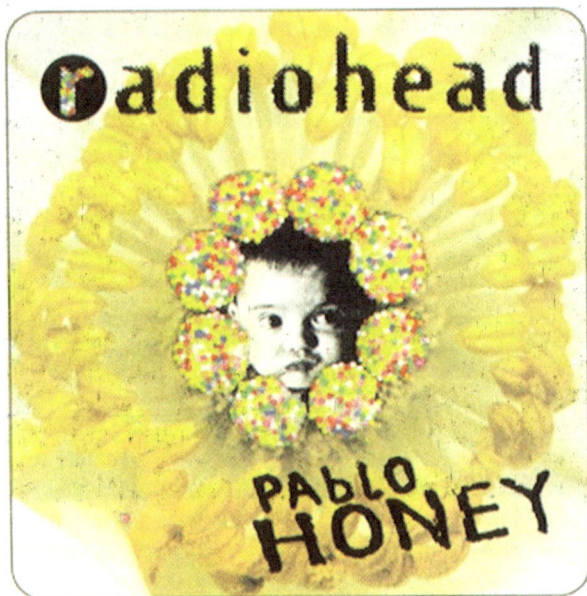

● ●

▼ Kid A *was released in 2000 and was partly promoted through the Internet.*

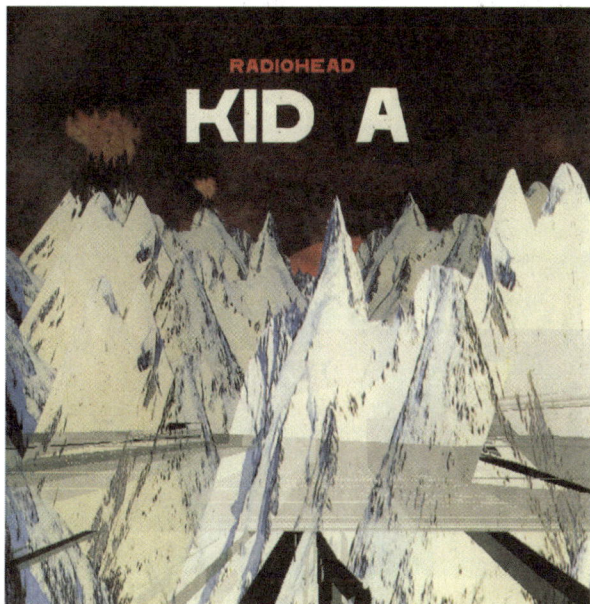

As the band began writing new songs for the album, singer Thom Yorke told *Time* magazine, 'I like the people at our record company, but the time is at hand when you have to ask why anyone needs one. And, yes, it probably would give us some perverse pleasure to say "F*** you" to this decaying business model.'

● ●

◄ Pablo Honey *was Radiohead's first album, released in 1993.*

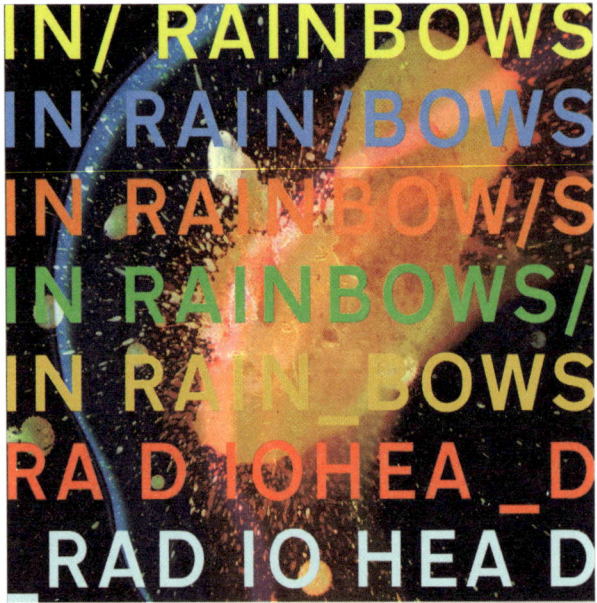

Radiohead retained ownership of the album recordings and song compositions for *In Rainbows*. The download and 'discbox' versions of the album (the box included a second enhanced CD with eight additional tracks, as well as digital photos and artwork, packaged in a hardcover book and slipcase) were self-released, while the band licensed the music to record labels worldwide for the later physical release.

◄ *Fans could download* In Rainbows *from Radiohead's website and pay whatever they felt the music was worth.*

HANDY HINTS

Think outside the box and brainstorm with your band members after a rehearsal. Only one in 20 ideas will be worth pursuing – but it could just be the one to make your name!

Radiohead declined to reveal Internet sales figures, but reported that 'most people (paid) a normal retail price with very few trying to buy (the download version) for a penny'. Its conventional retail release in December 2007/January 2008 saw *In Rainbows* enter the UK and Billboard chart at No. 1, the beneficiary of priceless publicity. (A total figure of three million physical/virtual copies was estimated.) The exercise demonstrated the power of the World Wide Web but was hardly a business plan a less-established band could follow.

▼ *Radiohead's website www.radiohead.com*

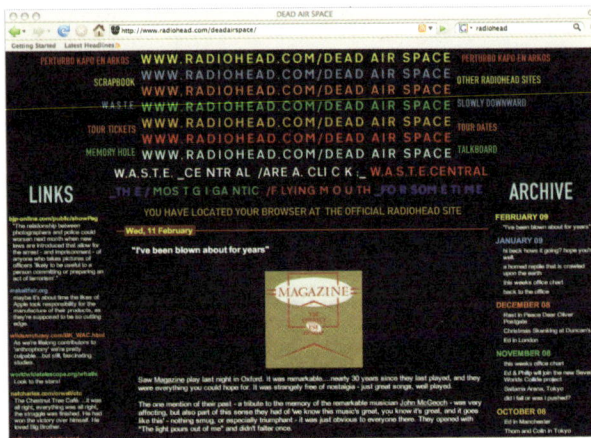

▶ *You could consider selling exclusively through your website to ensure you keep 100 per cent of the profits.*

HANDY HINTS

Signed merchandise and/or photographs are cheap 'add-ons' to music purchases that fans will value.

Other Success Stories

Jill Sobule

When the record company American singer-songwriter Jill Sobule was signed to went bust she used the Internet to ask fans for donations to produce, manufacture, distribute and promote a new album. In exchange for donations, she offered gifts ranging from a free download of the album when released ($10) to the opportunity to sing on the record ($10,000). In March 2008, 53 days after its launch, she had reached her $75,000 target through donations from over 500 people. As the album came together, Sobule used her blog to get opinions on song mixes, track order and album titles.

HANDY HINTS

Use the net to consult fans. If they feel they've played a part in choosing song titles, etc., they'll almost certainly buy the album.

▼ *Check out the website that Jill Sobule used to raise money to record an album, www.jillsnextrecord.com*

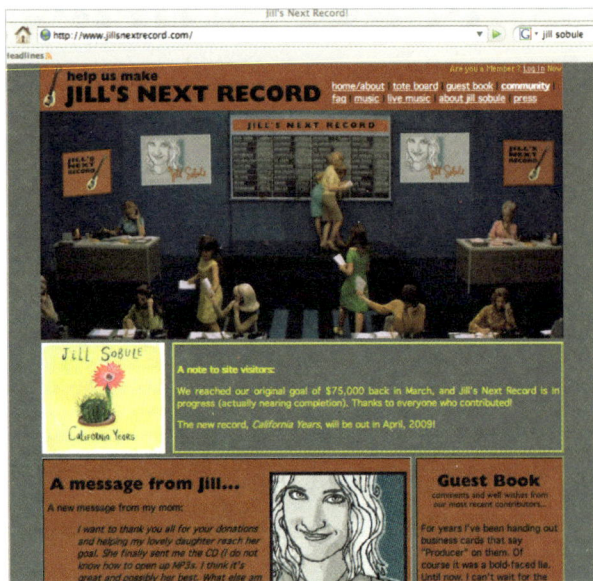

Kristin Hersh

Kristin Hersh, who made her name as a singer with Eighties US folk band Throwing Muses, created the ThrowingMusic label in 1996. This enabled her to release recordings, including a download subscription service called Works in Progress (WIP), exclusively through the label's ThrowingMusic website.

▼ *Kristin Hersh's website www.kristinhersh.com/*

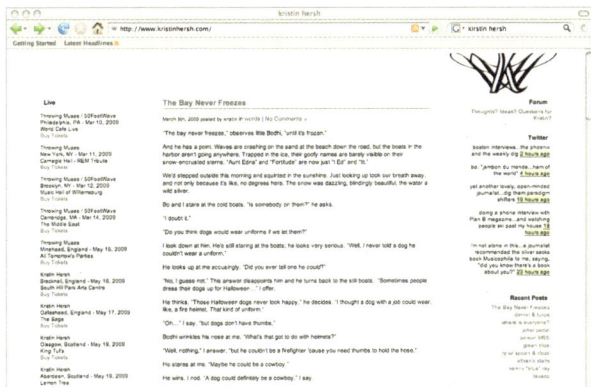

Sandi Thom

Scots-born singer-songwriter Sandi Thom broadcast gigs from her basement flat in Tooting, south London in 2006, announcing the gigs on her MySpace page. The venue had a capacity of 'six people' ('10 including the band').

▶ *Sandi Thom's single 'I Wish I Was A Punk Rocker (With Flowers In My Hair)' made No. 7 in the official downloads chart.*

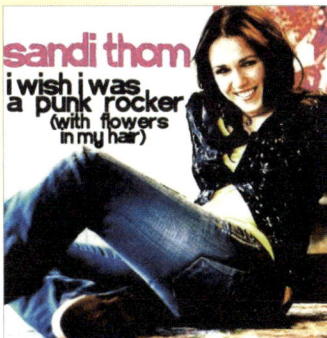

▼ *Sandi Thom's website www.sandithom.com*

The audience for the first day was around 60 or 70 and at its peak rose to a claimed 70,000. Her single 'I Wish I Was A Punk Rocker (With Flowers In My Hair)' made No. 15 on download sales and No. 7 in the UK official downloads chart, but when signed by Sony BMG records she found herself in June with a physical chart-topper.

Ian McNabb

In 2007 British singer-songwriter Ian McNabb (who came to fame two decades earlier with new-wave band Icicle Works) played an Internet tour of concerts in his supporters' living rooms.

'Round up the troops, get the food and booze in and I will rock your curtains,' he said. 'No rip-off ticket prices/overpriced drinks, no curfew, no parking problems. Your favourite artist delivered to your door!' It was a cheap way to promote his music without the need to hire venues; a real buzz developed on his fansites and everyone wanted to be in on the act.

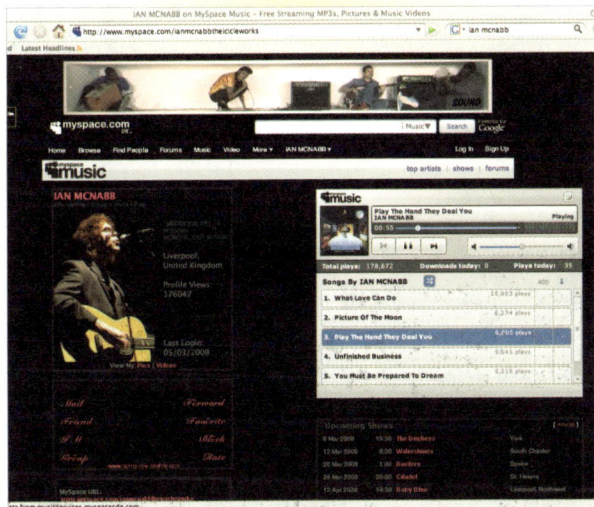

▲ *Ian McNabb's MySpace page.*

▲ *Lily Allen has used the Internet to find success as a musician.*

▼ *Lily Allen's website www.lilyallenmusic.com*

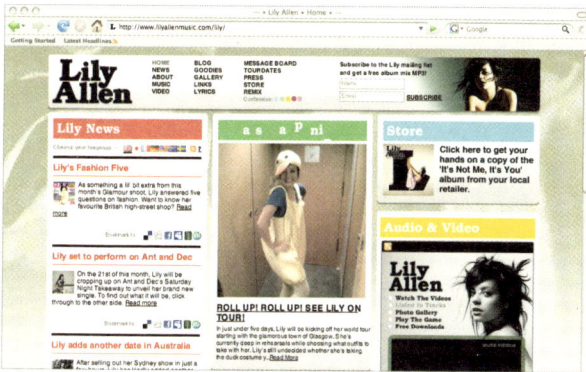

Lily Allen

Lily Allen is another such success story. After being frustrated by the slow pace of the record industry, Lily took things into her own hands; she created a MySpace page in November 2005 and started posting demos of her music, which immediately attracted thousands of listeners. Her first album *Alright, Still* (2006) was an instant hit and has sold over two million copies worldwide. Whilst working on her second album, *It's Not Me, It's You* (2009) she posted songs that were still works-in-progress so that fans could get an idea of the new direction her music was taking.

Summary

Check your progress against this list

Use viral marketing to promote your music
by giving exclusive music away to fans . . . . ☐

Introduce the new songs to your stage set so
those 'in the know' feel a part of your success . . . . . ☐

Offer fans limited editions and special
merchandise if they pay up-front. . . . . ☐

Consider selling exclusively through your website
to ensure you keep 100 per cent of the proceeds . . ☐

Release a free 'taster' track as an
MP3 download to whet the appetite. . . . . ☐

Publicize your innovative sales and promotion
tactics to the local and national media . . . . ☐

Be prepared to play a tiny living-room
venue to whip up enthusiasm – you
might even get a square meal out of it.
But remember to invite the neighbours!. . . . . ☐

GUIDE TO MUSIC ON THE WEB

The Internet has democratized music like never before. The resources available to listener and performer in the twenty-first century are almost limitless and changing and expanding by the day. This is a guide that will inevitably be out-of-date before you read it but many pointers will remain valid. So get clicking!

1
2
3
4
5
6
7
8
9
10
11
12

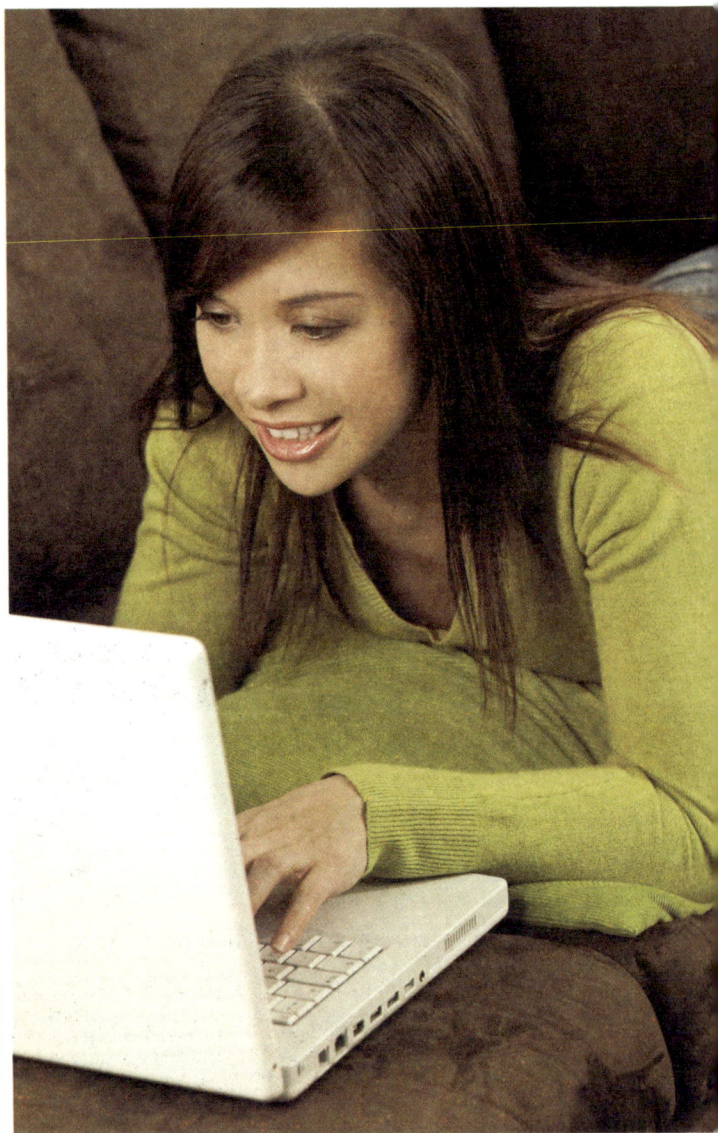

MUSIC SERVICES

Introduction

There are countless ways to consume music these days, and many of them are web-based. There are online radio stations, personalized streaming, online jukeboxes and download sites. Other sites let you share files, though these have not always operated legally, while online record stores like Amazon permit the sale of physical products that will arrive at your door as opposed to your modem. It's your choice!

There is also the opportunity, with many sites, to become part of a community of listeners who participate and communicate through the medium of music radio in a way never before possible. Read on and join in ...

11

Online Radio Stations

While most media is going digital, radio has remained resolutely analogue. Digital terrestrial and satellite radio services have remained the poor relation to analogue in terms of listeners. The advent of web-based radio has opened up a potential audience of almost 1.5 billion Internet users worldwide, of which two-thirds have broadband access. Furthermore, music-oriented communities are becoming social networks that let you share your listening preferences with your online buddies.

▲ *There is no need to listen to your old analogue radio anymore – go online!*

▼ *Many online radio stations, accessible through Live365, play niche genres of music seldom heard on traditional AM/FM radio.*

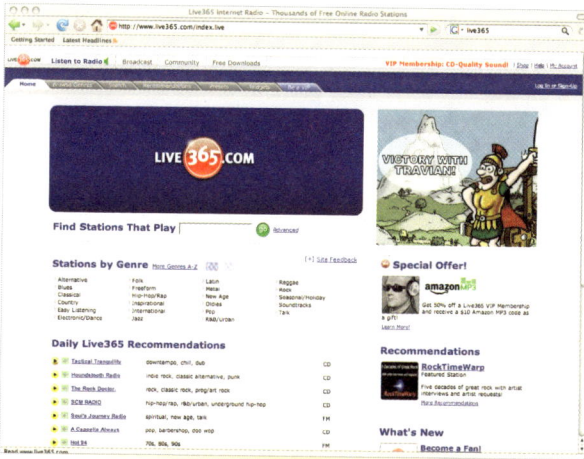

Online radio is most easily accessed via music-related websites like Live365. They provide access to thousands of web-based radio stations playing just about every conceivable kind of music. What differs is the variety of its offerings and the tools with which you access this multiplicity of choices.

You can access those programming options by searching via such criteria as artist, CD and track names, station names and descriptions, location by city or country and station category. You can use the

▼ *You can buy downloads from MSN Music and iTunes Music Store via Live 365.*

preset function to develop your own collection of favourite stations, while songs that catch your ear can be bookmarked by clicking on the icon located to the right of the displayed song name. This will add the song to your 'wish list'.

With Live365, Windows (PC) users have the option of buying downloads from either the iTunes Music Store or the MSN Music store, while Macintosh users can buy from the iTunes Music Store. Live365 also recommend new stations based on your preset lists.

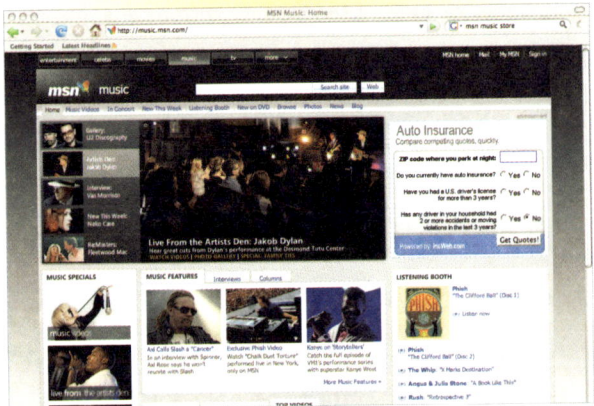

▼ *Listen to BBC Radio live online or 'listen again' via the BBC iPlayer.*

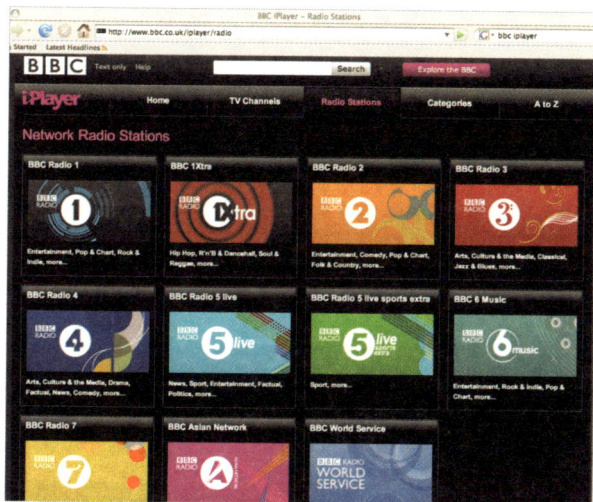

These are displayed on the 'my live365' page in the recommendations tab.

Live365 can be accessed free, but registration is required. A 'VIP Preferred Member' option provides ad-free listening and access to more stations in better quality. The United Kingdom has BBC Radio, a totally free service featuring a 'listen again' facility to access recent programming.

Personalized Radio & Interactive Streaming

While Internet radio can be consumed passively, as with its analogue ancestor, personalized radio sites like LAUNCHcast and last.fm encourage interaction and participation. Last.fm is a UK-based Internet radio and music community website, founded in 2002. It claims over 21 million active users based in more than 200 countries. In May 2007, it was acquired by CBS Interactive.

US-based LAUNCHcast has proved similarly successful. It broke through the 'two million listeners per week' mark in 2005, and provides a personalized music stream based on your rating of the music provided. You enter the names of favourite artists and music genres – then, as each song plays, your rating will influence what

▼ *Last.fm's music library contains well over 3.5 million audio tracks from artists on all the major commercial labels.*

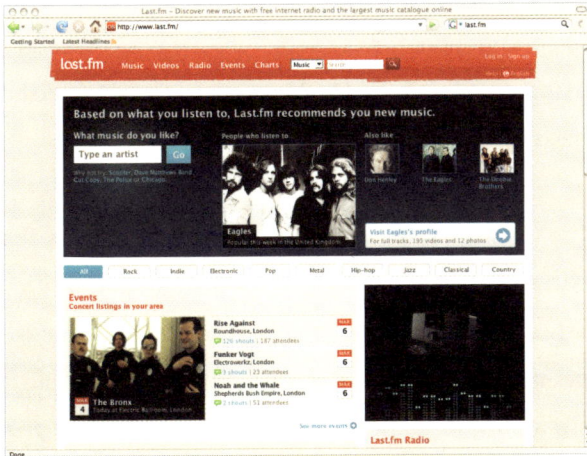

is later delivered. Songs, albums and artists can be rated on a star scale of zero (lowest) to four (highest). The more songs you rate, the better your profile becomes and the more likely you are to enjoy what gets played.

LAUNCHcast also provides over 100 pre-programmed stations, offering different genres, themes and eras, plus stations that play music from one particular artist or family of artists. While listening, you can click on the linked names of artists, songs and albums

▼ *Rate the music you listen to on LAUNCHcast and your rating will influence what is played.*

for information, and can communicate with other fans using Yahoo Instant Messenger, artist-focused messageboards and a LAUNCHcast user group.

The service is offered as free and paid-for options, the latter (LAUNCHcast Plus) offering unlimited ad-free listening as opposed to the free version's 600-songs-per-month allocation. You get higher quality music streams and unlimited skipping, plus more pre-programmed music stations.

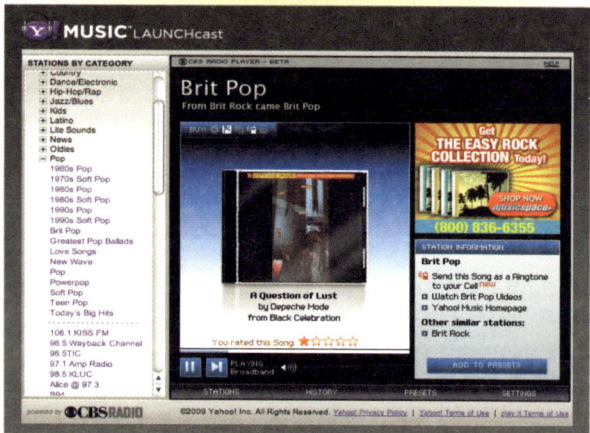

One drawback of LAUNCHcast is the lack of a stand-alone desktop player application. It relies on Internet Explorer, though another option is to use the player built into Yahoo's Messenger instant messaging application. LAUNCHcast was bought by Yahoo in 2001 and combined with CBS Radio in February 2009. This relaunch made it available to Firefox and Macintosh users.

▲ *www.musicovery.com is another interactive online radio station.*

▼ *LAUNCHcast was bought by Yahoo in 2001 and combined with CBS Radio in February 2009.*

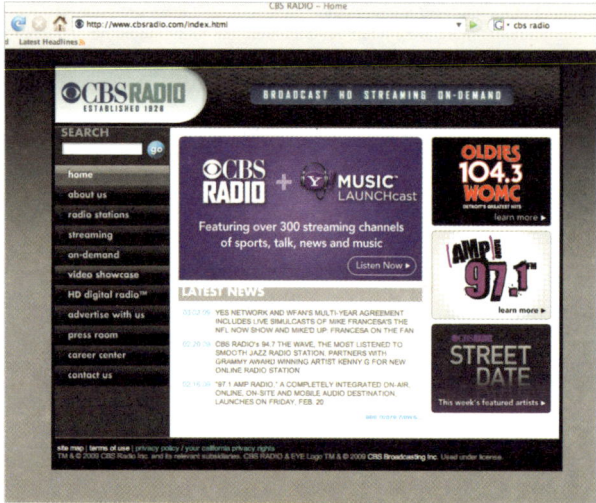

Mention should also be made of MOG, a social networking site where computer users can set up personal pages with their musical interests and listening history. There are tools for connecting with other similar users. MOG is similar to Last.fm, but it first uploads a listing of a user's digital music collection to their MOG page, then keeps track of what music is played on the user's computer.

Online Jukeboxes

On-demand music services known as online jukeboxes are also called streaming services. They provide unlimited access to a huge library of music and, for a monthly fee, you can listen to as many songs and albums as you like.

▲ *Streamwaves is an online jukebox that works well on both Macs and PCs.*

With the likes of Musicmatch, Rhapsody and Napster giving you access to more albums than you could afford to buy, the online jukebox service is invaluable for those wanting to increase their knowledge of music. Most of these services use software that only runs on PCs operating Windows. Streamwaves is the exception, its web interface equally effective on both PCs and Apple Macintosh computers.

HANDY HINTS

If subscribing to an online jukebox site, pay attention not only to the size of the catalogue offered, but also to its scope. What types of artists and music are included? Check the coverage in your particular areas of interest.

Musicmatch, founded in 1997 and based in San Diego, claimed to have invented the digital jukebox concept in 1997, and since then has registered more than 28 million users of its number-one-selling Musicmatch Jukebox service. This was based on an extensive catalogue from major music labels including artists such as Eminem, Pink Floyd and U2. Today, Musicmatch

HANDY HINTS

If the digital music marketplace is just too confusing, ask your friends for their experiences of online music, and follow up their personal recommendations.

MX customers can create artist-based playlists from more than 8,000 artists and 20,000 albums, and the list continues to grow each week.

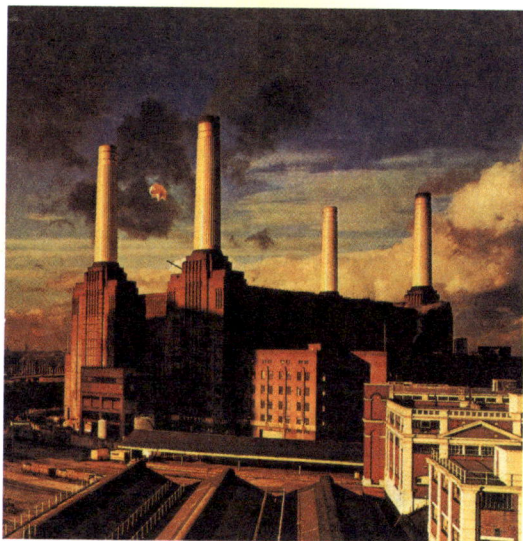

▲ *Musicmatch has an extensive catalogue including artists such as Pink Floyd.*

11

Rhapsody & Napster

Rhapsody subscribers can burn selected tracks to CDs in CD audio format, making them playable in any CD player and available for 'ripping' into MP3 files. This service is only available in the United States, however, and some copyright holders will allow a song to be played but not burned to CD. You can bookmark songs, albums and radio stations for later use as well as assembling playlists for playing or CD-burning.

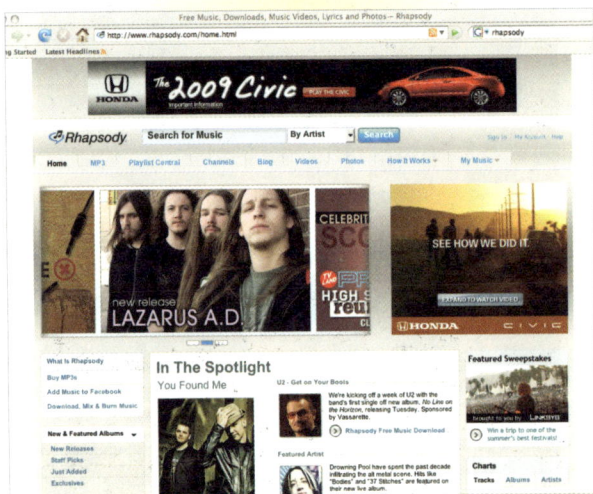

▲ *Rhapsody was the first streaming on-demand music subscription service to offer unlimited access to its entire library of digital music for a flat monthly fee.*

Rhapsody has a big catalogue of major label and independent music and its unlimited access for a flat monthly fee is good for adventurous users, but on the down side there are no messageboards or forums for music sharing between fans.

Napster, once an illegal file-sharing operation, is now very much a legal service offering more than seven million tracks covering every genre from the mainstream to the obscure. It offers three levels of service: Napster Light (downloads), Napster Unlimited (unlimited music for a flat fee) and Napster To Go which allows unlimited music transfer to a compatible player for a higher monthly membership fee. These can be burned to CD for an extra charge, but the real attraction is the ability to listen on the move.

HANDY HINTS

Many Internet-based services offer free trial periods – well worth taking up on a 'try before you buy' basis. But don't forget to cancel your direct debit after the initial period or they will charge you.

MP3 Download Sites

Apple's iTunes Music Store launched in 2003 and introduced millions of us to the concept of buying downloads online. iTunes software is well designed and simple to use, allowing the user to download music to their hard disk and transfer files to and from Apple's iPod portable music player, as well as burning CDs.

▲ *iTunes software is well designed and simple to use.*

HANDY HINTS

In an historic move, DRM (Digital Rights Management) was dropped by iTunes in January 2009, allowing the ability to transfer files without restriction – and, though not widely realized, better quality music to be offered.

Apple offers in excess of one million tracks from every major and the majority of independent labels from its easy-to-use download store. No subscription is required. Other services have arrived that offer cheaper downloads, but iTunes remains a standard. It has recently (early 2009) stared to offer files without DRM rights protection, which has made manipulating and using your collection much easier.

HANDY HINTS

If you purchase a CD, make sure the disc does not come with DRM technology that prevents you from copying the tracks to a computer if you wish to use it either there or on a portable device.

▼ *You can download the iTunes software for free and do not need to subscribe – you only pay to download the tracks that you want.*

HANDY HINTS

Make sure the file format of the music you are downloading is compatible with the device you want to play it on – e.g. iPod or MP3 player. There's nothing more frustrating than a compatibility problem. iTunes customers who want to use a player other than an iPod or iPhone may still have to transcode the songs into MP3, but iTunes can now do this for you.

Musicmatch offers music downloads, via its music store, as well as radio and its previously mentioned jukebox service. Music discovered while listening to Musicmatch's radio and on-demand services can also be purchased. Unlike Napster, however, Musicmatch doesn't have messageboards or a forum for users to share recommendations. It does, however, provide an all-in-one music solution, being an Internet radio, online jukebox and downloading service (its downloads won't work with Apple's iPod portable music players, however).

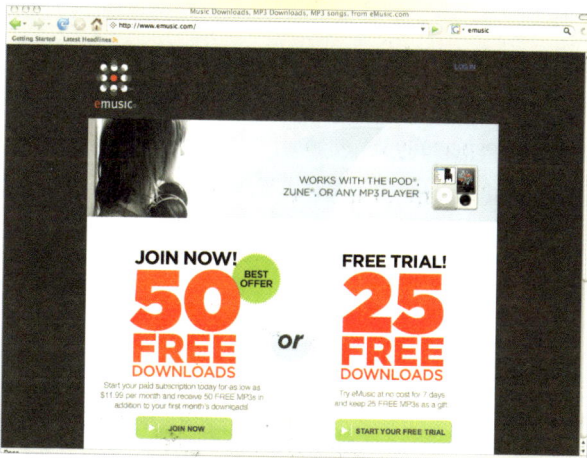

▲ *Most of eMusic's contracts are with independent labels, leading it to specialize in underground artists and non-mainstream music genres.*

HANDY HINTS

Do you want to buy music or be part of a community? If the latter, look specifically for music websites that offer messageboards or forums to post your views.

eMusic is a subscription-based service with a catalogue of over 750,000 tracks from over 31,000 artists. It is based on independent labels and so charges less per track than many mainstream services. eMusic's downloads in the MP3 format can be played on almost any portable music player, while messageboards allow you to discuss music with other subscribers. eMusic requires you to spend a minimum sum a month but represents good value – especially as if you lose your files or want to download them to another computer, they will not count against your monthly allocation of tracks provided your subscription is active.

. . . .
▶ *eMusic's files are not DRM encoded so can be played on almost any portable music player.*

File-sharing Sites

The first and most famous file-sharing site, Napster was the brainchild of student Shawn Fanning from Boston who, using his knowledge of programming, created a decentralized, easily distributed programme that would allow users to share music and other files over the Internet on a peer-to-peer (P2P) basis – i.e. between individual users' computers. There was no central server, it was the equivalent of swapping music directly with friends.

▲ Napster; the first and most famous file-sharing site.

343

Unfortunately this was done without paying royalties to the copyright holder and incurred the wrath of many industry figures, including heavy rockers Metallica who were particularly vocal in their complaints. Napster was liquidated in 2002, the name being later purchased by Roxio for a legitimate download service to capitalize on the popularity of the former service.

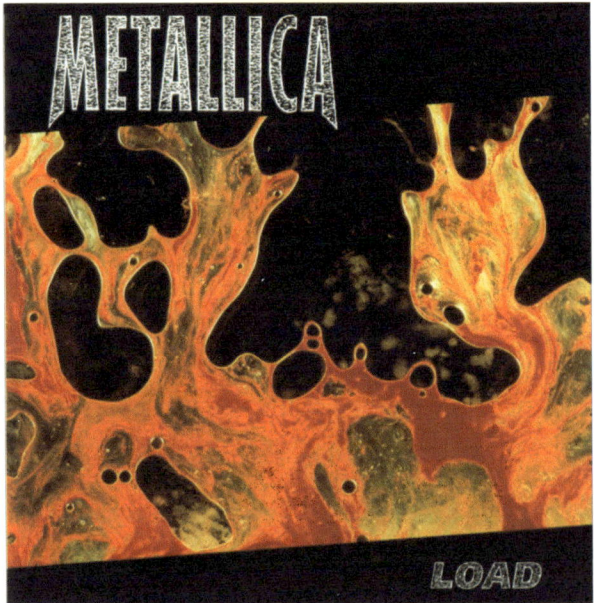

▲ *In 2000, Metallica was among several artists who filed a lawsuit against Napster for sharing the band's copyright-protected material for free without the band members' consent.*

P2P Networks

P2P file-sharing networks still exist, mostly for the sharing of live performance recordings, and some of the most popular are listed below. But be warned: while using P2P technology isn't illegal, copyright infringement is. So no liability is accepted should you use any of the below.

PIRATE BAY

A Swedish-based site which, with over 2.8 million registered users and in excess of one million active torrents, is the largest file-sharing database on the web.

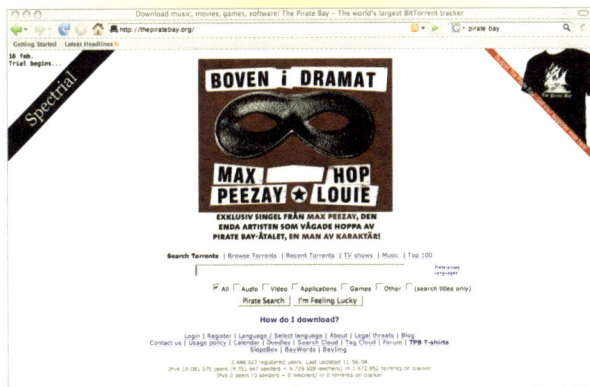

▲ *Pirate Bay was ranked as the 107th most popular website by Alexa Internet in 2009.*

MININOVA

Born after the first reincarnation of SuprNova was shut down in 2004, MiniNova offers over 35 music genres and has a good search engine with advanced options.

▲ *MiniNova was started in January 2005 and is based in the Netherlands.*

ISOHUNT

A BitTorrent indexing site based in Canada. Its search feature is basic and doesn't compare with that offered by, say, MiniNova but a simple layout makes it easy to use.

▼ *IsoHunt, like many file-sharing websites, has faced lawsuits over copyright infringement.*

BITTORRENT.AM

One of the newer and most popular P2P file-sharing websites. There are over 600,000 torrents indexed, divided into over 45 different genres.

▼ *BitTorrent.am; a new and popular file-sharing site.*

TORRENT PORTAL

Not only has this a user-friendly interface with good advanced search facilities, you can also see what other users have searched for among over 1.4 million torrents on offer.

▲ *Over 400,000 torrents are uploaded on to Torrent Portal daily.*

Online Record Stores

While much music is now downloaded via the Internet, there are still many people who prefer the physical solidity of the compact disc. There are many stores who can deliver CDs direct to the door in less than 24 hours, and most also now offer downloads.

The most famous online record store is Amazon.com, founded by Jeff Bezos in 1994 and launched in 1995. It started life as a bookstore but soon diversified to

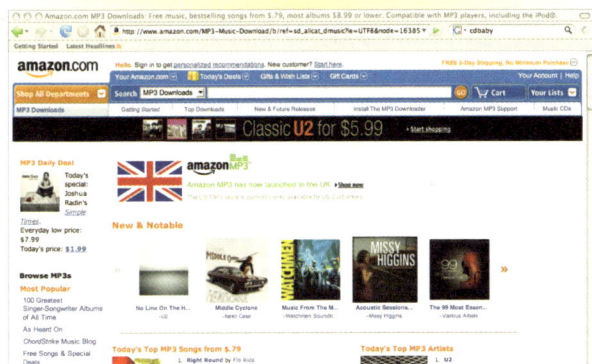

▲ *www.amazon.com is America's largest online retailer.*

▼ *CD Baby allows independent musicians to sell directly to consumers.*

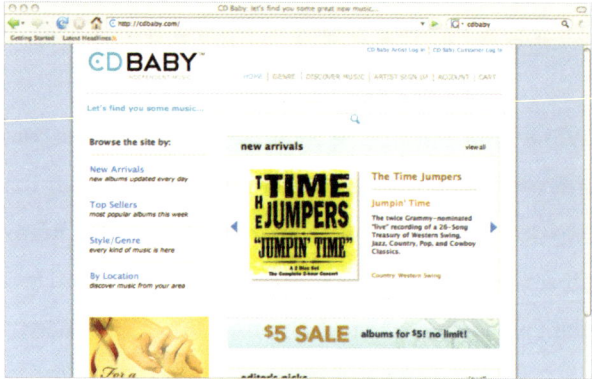

include music CDs. The Amazon MP3 Store was launched in September 2007 and is now the biggest rival to iTunes. The music has always been DRM (Digital Rights Management) free, meaning it can be used without restriction. Amazon MP3 sells music from all the major record labels as well as many independents.

CD Baby was founded by Derek Sivers in 1997 and sold in 2008 for $22 million to Disc Makers. It was founded to allow independent musicians to sell music directly to consumers. Artists set their price for selling physical compact discs, CD Baby retaining $4 of every sale; the remainder is paid to the artist on a weekly basis.

Among the 250,000 artists to have used CD Baby in the past are Jack Johnson, Gary Jules (of Mad World fame) and *American Idol* contestant Jordin Sparks.

HMV, the international retailer, is the largest of its kind in the UK and Canada. The initials stand for His Master's Voice and its history dates back to 1921, when the first HMV shop opened in London. The company has an online store to augment its 379 shops and in September 2008 launched its own social networking site, Get Closer. With its enviable resources and buying power it will undoubtedly be a major player in the future.

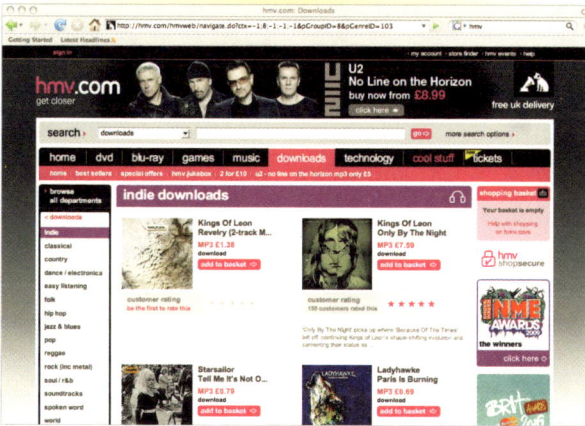

▲ *The HMV website was launched in 1997.*

Summary

Addresses of main sites mentioned in this section

Live 365 – www.live365.com . . . . ☐

BBC – www.bbc.co.uk/iplayer/radio . . . . ☐

LAUNCHcast –
music.launch.com/launchcast/ . . . . ☐

last.fm – www.last.fm . . . . ☐

Musicmatch – www.musicmatch.com . . . . ☐

Rhapsody – www.rhapsody.com . . . . ☐

Napster – www.napster.com . . . . ☐

Streamwaves – www.streamwaves.com . . . . ☐

iTunes – www.apple.com/itunes . . . . ☐

eMusic – www.emusic.com . . . . ☐

Amazon – http://www.amazon.com,
www.amazon.co.uk . . . . ☐

CD Baby – www.cdbaby.com . . . . ☐

HMV – http://www.hmv.com . . . . ☐

PRESS & RECORD LABELS

Introduction

Things happen so fast in music today that monthly music magazines simply can't react quickly enough. The best websites are traditionally based on established 'brands' of magazine, but their readership now far exceeds that of their physical counterpart. There are also sites to help you find details of managers, producers and record labels, all of which may well play a part in your future success. The divide between performers and listeners has been shrunk by the Internet to the point that you can not only choose what you want to listen to 24/7 but also communicate with fellow fans via forums and messageboards. The possibilities really are endless.

1
2
3
4
5
6
7
8
9
10
11
12

Guide To Music E-zines

The day of the 'inky' weekly music paper is long gone. Only the *New Musical Express* survives, but even the *NME* has an innovative website pointing the way to the future.

▲ *Find out all the latest news about your favourite musicians, like Lenny Kravitz, online.*

New Musical Express
www.nme.com

Launched in 1996, nme.com is currently Europe's most successful music website with 15 million page impressions per month and 1.2 million users. It is the digital archive of the *New Musical Express* music paper, founded in 1952, with over 15,000 news stories, reviews and features in its database. Over 20 new stories are added per day, covering the biggest and newest talent. In 2001 nme.com was voted 'Website of the Year' for the second time.

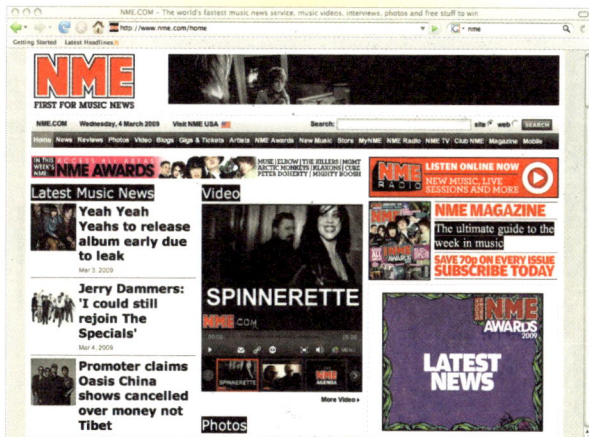

▲ *www.nme.com features news, photos, videos, blogs, reviews, gig listings, downloads and messageboards.*

Q
www.q4music.com

Q, the self-appointed 'World's Greatest Music Magazine', has a long-established web presence that continues the good work done by the magazine since 1986 when it was launched as Britain's answer to *Rolling Stone*. Regular readers will recognize the format, and the navigation is as easy as flicking the pages of the glossy parent magazine.

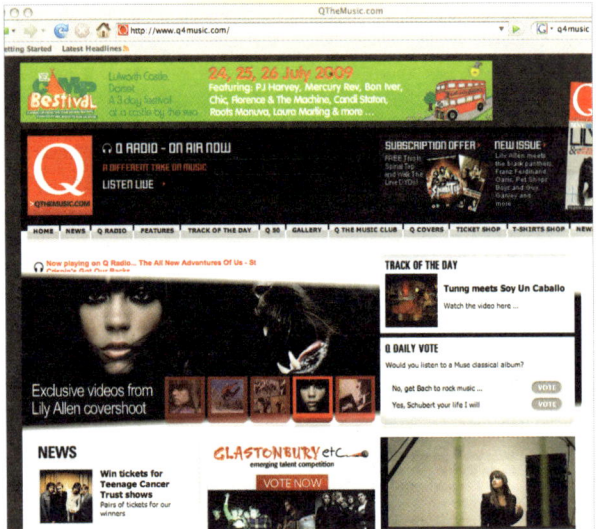

▲ *www.q4music.com has a long-established web presence.*

▲ *Whatever type of music you are into, there will be an e-zine for you.*

Mojo
www.mojo4music.com

The site was registered in 2000 as the online representative of *Mojo*, first published in 1993 and acclaimed as 'The world's most respected and authoritative rock magazine'. Less contemporary than *Q*, but still worthwhile.

▲ *www.mojo4music.com includes news and features on classic rock acts.*

Rolling Stone
www.rollingstone.com

The online version of *Rolling Stone* magazine includes music reviews, movie reviews, musical artists, free MP3s and photos. Subject-matter ranges from Britney Spears and Katy Perry through traditional artists to the indie scene, while the reviews section is authoritative.

▲ *The* Rolling Stone *record reviews section is regarded by many sources as one of the most influential.*

The Wire
www.thewire.co.uk

The Wire magazine, subtitled Adventures in Modern Music, published its 300th issue in 2009. Its website includes information from the print magazine plus breaking music news and events, and links to relevant sites.

▲ The Wire *initially concentrated on contemporary jazz and improvised music, but has branched out to cover various types of experimental music including post-rock, hip hop, modern classical, free improvisation and various forms of electronic music.*

Sound On Sound
www.soundonsound.com

Claiming to be 'the World's Best Music Recording Magazine', *SoS* and sister publication *Sound Pro* magazine are a must for anyone interested in recording technology. This website reflects their position as leaders in the field.

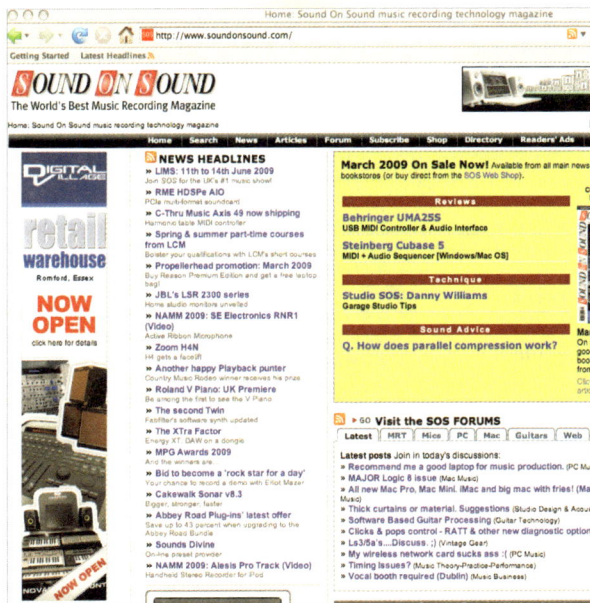

▲ Sound On Sound *is a must for anyone interested in recording technology.*

Check out these other good music e-zines:

☆ www.kerrang.com (rock)

☆ www.frootsmag.com (roots, folk and world)

☆ www.jazzwise.com (jazz)

☆ www.bbcmusicmagazine.com (classical)

☆ www.kmag.co.uk (drum and bass)

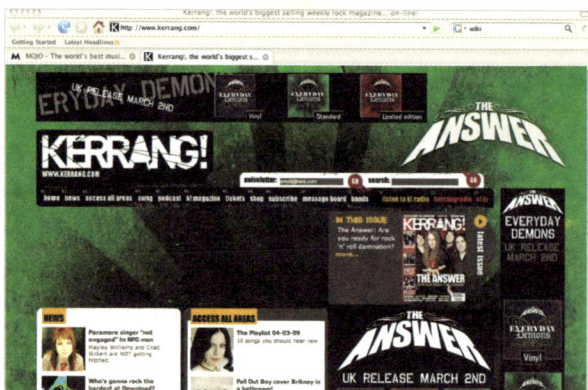

▲ *www.kerrang.com is the website of the world's biggest-selling rock magazine.*

HANDY HINTS

Write a press release for your own band, highlighting your newsworthiness, that a magazine website might publish. It's good practice for the future.

Finding Managers

Appointing a manager can be a tricky business. Get it right and you'll soon see the benefit. Get it wrong and it could cripple your band's career.

▲ *Go online to find a manager for your band.*

12

Music Managers Forum
www.musicmanagersforum.co.uk

The MMF provides a thought-provoking guide as to when you should get a manager – 'Generally, the sooner the better' – and what to look for as you make your choice. 'The artist/manager relationship is just like any other personal relationship – some relationships last forever, some for just a short while. The purpose of this (site) is merely to give you some guidance in the decision-making process.'

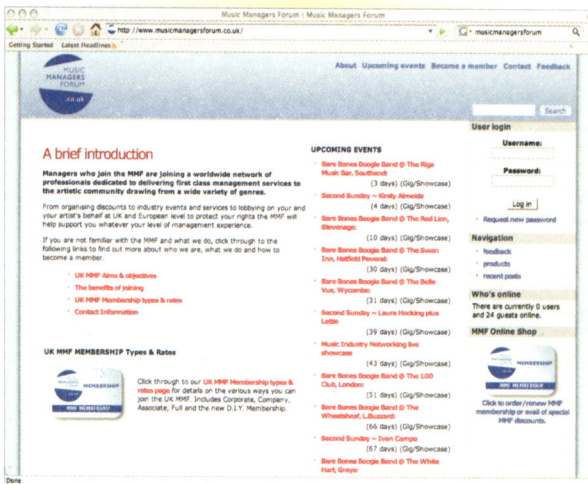

▲ *Use the MMF's guide to help you select the right manager for your band.*

MusicBizAdvice
www.musicbizadvice.com

A 'how to' guide containing advice from music industry professionals from local to international level that claims to have readers in 77 countries. Has more to advise you on than just what kind of manager to look for. American-based, but well worth a look.

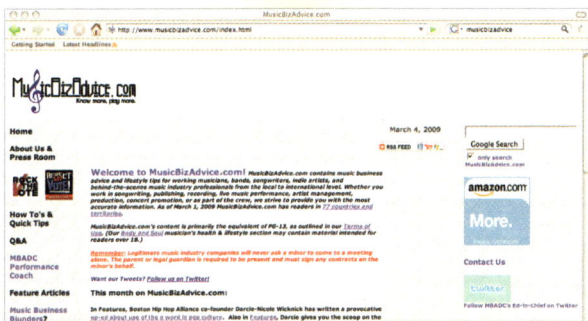

▲ *Packed with all sorts of information, www.musicbizadvice.com is a great read.*

HANDY HINTS

Never, ever sign an agreement – management, record label or otherwise – without taking independent legal advice. The time and expense may well pay you back in future.

Music Week
www.musicweek.com

Music Week magazine updates their online directory on an ongoing basis throughout the year to ensure that it is as accurate and up-to-date as possible. The magazine is a weekly that everyone in the UK record business reads, so all the relevant management contacts will be listed in their online directory with email addresses, postal addresses and even contact names. Only problem is you need to be a subscriber...

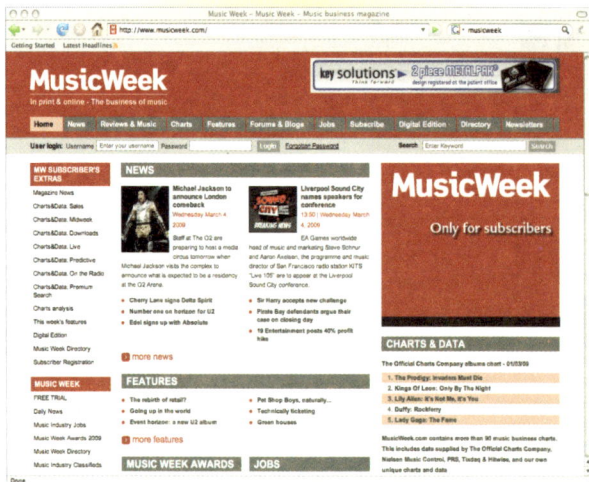

▲ *Consider subscribing to* Music Week *magazine – all the relevant management contacts are listed and up-to-date.*

Sonicbids
www.sonicbids.com

Musicians can hook up with potential managers, promoters, booking agents and industry professionals who are also members of the community site by submitting a bid, including an online press kit with audio and video tracks, photos and a biography. Musicians pay a monthly or annual membership fee, but a free trial period is offered. US-based.

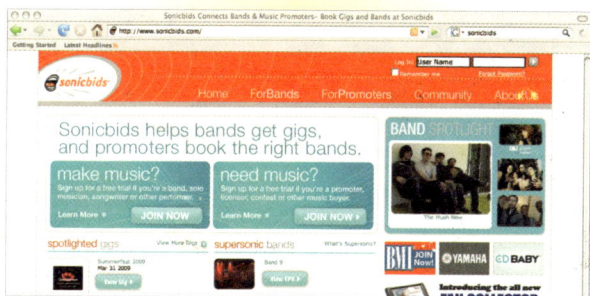

▲ *Submit an online press kit to potential managers via www.sonicbids.com*

HANDY HINTS

Do you need a manager, or a booking agent? Write out a list of what you want before you spend valuable time looking.

12

Finding Producers

You may have written your own songs and lugged your own gear around on the gig circuit, but when it comes to recording it can pay to have a professional producer to sweeten your sound.

▲ *Finding a great producer can make all the difference to the sound of your music.*

Studio Expresso
www.studioexpresso.com

The self-proclaimed 'Artists' gateway to the world's top music makers' offers clickable producer profiles and playable samples of new music with producer details highlighted. Also offers a free monthly newsletter, sent from sunny California.

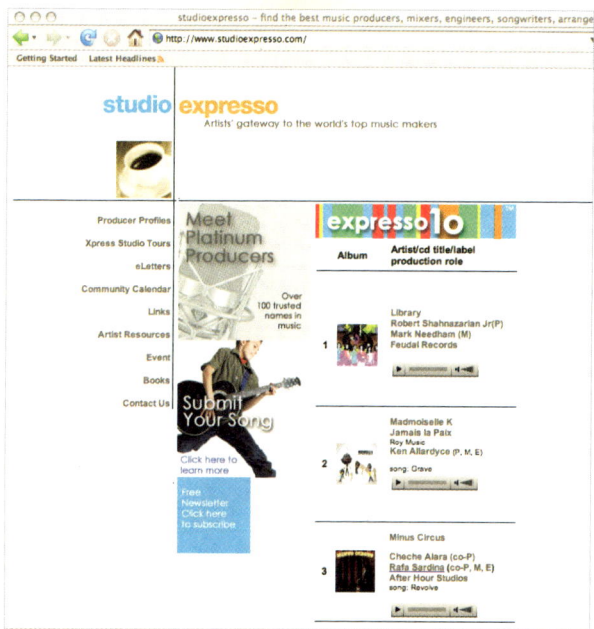

▲ *Sign up for Studio Expresso's free monthly newsletter.*

820
www.820m.com

American-based one-stop shop with lofty ambitions. 'Do you and your band have what it takes to make it big? Maybe you do, but chances are you don't. But for those of you that can make it to the next level, 820 works with you to find and negotiate the best possible record deal for your band. From marketing and promotion to production and recording – we give you the resources needed to become great.'

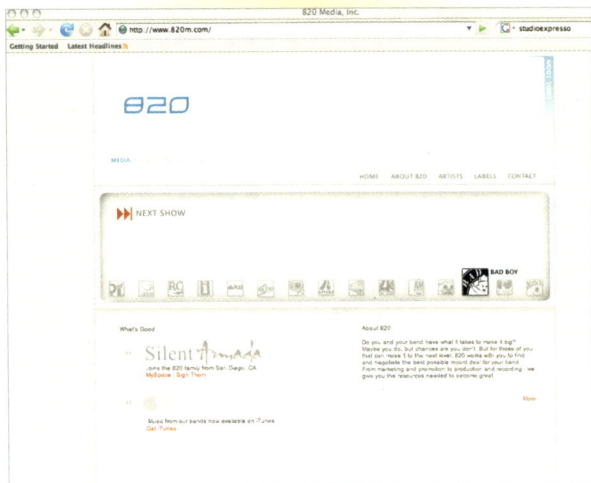

▲ *Why not upload a demo of your work to www.820m.com and see what happens?*

Music Producers Guild
www.mpg.org.uk/members

The Music Producers Guild represents the interests of UK record producers, music recording engineers, mixers and everyone directly involved in the production of recorded music. It's mainly concerned with record-making and recording techniques for all genres of music in the UK, but has a searchable database of members and their contact details.

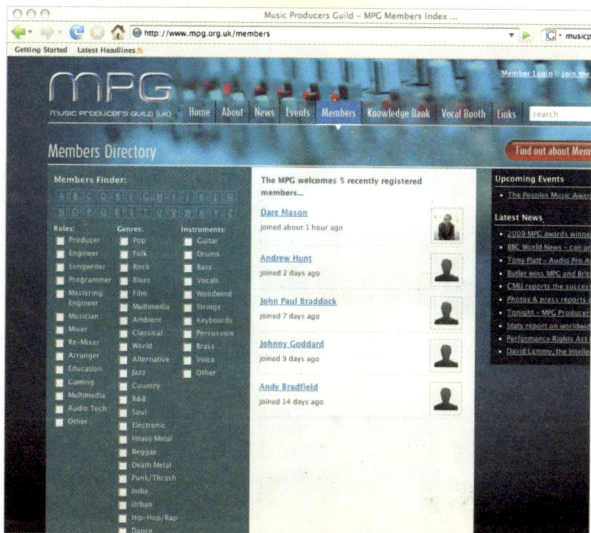

▲ *The Music Producers Guild has a searchable database of members and their contact details.*

Finding Record Labels

So, you've put together a great band, had a professional demo recorded and hired yourself a good manager. Now time to get that elusive record deal with a major label? Here's how to find them....

▲ *Sony Music is one of the 'Big Four' record companies.*

Wikipedia
http://en.wikipedia.org/wiki/
list_of_record_labels

Good old Wikipedia is your first stop. It lists major record labels from A–Z, with clickable links that will take you to pages with the details you need.

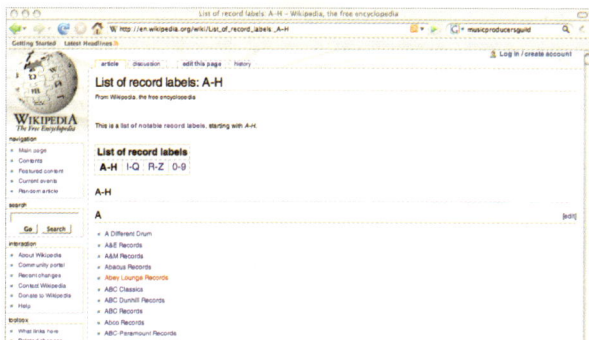

▲ *Wikipedia lists major record labels from A–Z.*

HANDY HINTS

Check out the 'happening' record labels whose bands are breaking through and being featured on music press sites. Find out more about them from the 'finding record labels' sites and compile a 'hit list' to approach.

Music Week
www.musicweek.com

As with finding a manager, the UK music industry weekly *Music Week* is the one with all the details. You have to be a subscriber to gain full access to their comprehensive online directory of contacts, spanning the whole industry with more than 10,000 entries. But it might be worth investigating – or, totally unethically, finding a subscriber who might take a look for you!

▲ *Search* Music Week*'s directory of contacts online.*

▲ *Richard Branson founded the famous Virgin Records label in 1972. It is now owned by EMI.*

12

All Record Labels
http://allrecordlabels.com/
db/genres/

A listing that features not only labels but genres of music, so you have the best chance of finding a label that has a track record in what you do. Clicking reveals a list of label names, which gives way to individual profiles and then takes you to the label's website. It does almost everything for you but send the demo CD!

▲ *A record label's website is just a few clicks away on http://allrecordlabels.com*

HANDY HINTS

If you're writing your own songs and intend to release them you'll also need to have a music publisher (separate from a record label). For basic advice, see http://www.copynot.org

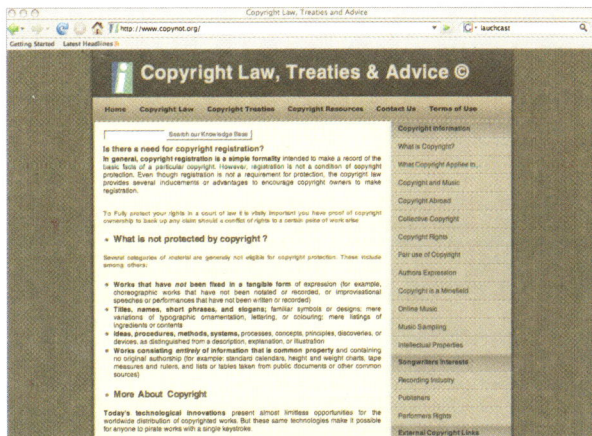

▲ *www.copynot.com provides basic copyright advice.*

HANDY HINTS

Do you really need a record label yet – or at all? Investigate the possibility of selling your music off your website/MySpace page and at gigs.

12

Summary

A list of useful site addresses mentioned in this section

Music E-zines:

www.nme.com .... ☐

www.q4music.com .... ☐

www.mojo4music.com .... ☐

www.rollingstone.com.......................... ☐

www.thewire.co.uk .... ☐

www.soundonsound.com........................ ☐

Managers:

www.musicmanagersforum.co.uk .... ☐

www.musicbizadvice.com .... ☐

www.musicweek.com .... ☐

www.sonicbids.com .... ☐

Producers:

www.studioexpresso.com........................ ☐

www.82om.com .... ☐

www.mpg.org.uk/members .... ☐

Record Labels:

http://en.wikipedia.org/wiki/list_of_record_labels .. ☐

www.musicweek.com .... ☐

http://allrecordlabels.com/db/genres/ .... ☐

Author Biographies

Ronan Macdonald (Foreword)

Ronan Macdonald has worked as a technical music journalist since 1989. He has written features and reviews as a freelance contributor to a plethora of magazines, including *Future Music*, *The Mix*, *Hip-Hop Connection* and *Guitarist*. He has also occupied the editor's chair on *Rhythm*, the UK's leading drummer magazine, and currently edits *Computer Music*, the world's only dedicated music software magazine. A rusty drummer and fanatical home studio rat, Ronan firmly believes that everyone has an inner musician waiting to be freed by a book like this one.

Michael Heatley (Author)

Michael Heatley has written over 100 books, has penned liner notes to more than 100 CD reissues, and written for magazines including *Music Week*, *Billboard*, *Goldmine*, *Radio Times* and *Record Collector*. More recently he was the author of *How To Write Great Songs*, *How To Play Hard, Metal & Nu Rock* and *How To Play Rock Rhythm, Riffs & Lead*, also published by Flame Tree.

Alan Kinsman (Contributor)

Alan Kinsman is a musician and author who has written sleeve notes for many prestigious album releases from the 1980s to the present. He has also contributed to a number of music and history-related books.

Further Reading

Baker, B., *MySpace Music Marketing: How To Promote & Sell Your Music on the World's Biggest Networking Web Site*, Bob Baker, 2006

Beall, E., *Making Music Make Money*, Berklee Press Publications, 2007

Fries, B., *The MP3 and Internet Audio Handbook: Your Guide to the Digital Music Revolution*, Teamcom Books, 2000

Gallagher, M., *Mastering Music at Home: How to Master Your Recordings for CD and Web Distribution*, Delmar, 2007

Gilby, C., *MP3 and the Infinite Digital Jukebox*, Seven Stories Press, 2001

Gordon, S., *Future of the Music Business: How to Succeed with the New Digital Technologies*, Hal Leonard Corporation, 2008

Griencewic, R., *Use Your PC to Explore Digital Music*, Gateway Press, 2003

Hill, B., *Digital Songstream: Mastering the World of Digital Music*, Routledge, 2003

Johnson, D. and Broida, R., *How To Do Everything with MP3 and Digital Music*, Osborne/McGraw-Hill, 2001

Kalliongis, N., *MySpace Music Profit Monster!: And All Proven Online Music Marketing Strategies!*, Booksurge, 2007

Mewton, C., *Music and the Internet Revolution*, Sanctuary Publishing, 2001

Nevue, D., *How To Promote Your Music Successfully on the Internet*, Booksurge, 2008

Simmons, M., *Creating a Music Website*, PC Publishing, 2001

Sparrow, A., *Music Distribution and the Internet: A Legal Guide for the Music Business*, Gower Publishing Ltd, 2006

Spellman, P., *The Musician's Internet: On-line Strategies for Success in the Music Industry*, Berklee Press Publications, 2002

Wiedemann, J. (ed.), *Web Design: Music Sites*, Taschen, 2006

Picture Credits

Courtesy of **Shutterstock** and the following photographers: 61, 117; Mohannad Fariz Abdullah: 48; Victoria Alexandrova: 301; Mark Allchin: 175; Vartanov Anatoly: 143; AndreiC: 62 (b); Szymon Apanowicz: 173; Tim Arbaev: 37; Yuri Arcurs: 178, 213; Andrey Arkusha: 57 (b); Darren Baker: 322; Rick Becker-Leckrone: 133 (b); Atanas Bezov: 277; blackan: 156; blueking: 321; Corky Buczyk: 57 (t); Ryan Carter: 24; Konstantin Chagin: 241; Brian Chase: 88; Ivan Cholakov: 285, 374; Chunni4691: 56; H.D. Connelly: 99; Lugosi Dániel: 73; Phil Date: 242; Digital Sport Photoagency: 65; djem: 310 (b); Maslov Dmitry: 276; Dooley Productions: 21; Michael Drager: 324; DW Photos: 45; Entertainment Press: 316; Ermek: 166, 286; Marie C. Fields: 32; Miodrag Gajic: 319; Adam Gasson: 190; Gemenacom: 43; Sony Ho: 171; Richard Hoffart: 342; HP Photo: 67; David Hughes: 106; Charlie Hutton: 59; Mostovyi Sergii Igorevich: 93; Dusan Jankovic: 255; JJJ: 18; Alexander Kalina: 164; Karkas: 55; Laitr Keiows: 111; konstantynov: 100; kret87: 35; Magdalena Kucova: 270; Jesse Kunerth: 118; Robert Kyllo: 51; Jim Lopes: 353; Vilena Makarica: 356; F. Mann: 167; Mark Stout Photography: 26; Dmitry Melnikov: 108; Svetlana Mihailova: 147 (l); Robert Milek: 294; MilousSK: 54 (t); mirounga: 58; Morgan Lane Photography: 159, 165; Juriah Mosin: 269; Muellek: 182; Ariusz Nawrocki: 359; Nic Neish: 63; Micael António Maria Nussbaumer: 17; olly: 256; Orpheus: 86, 177; Amra Pasic: 246; PHOTOCREO: Michal Bednarek: 293; photomak: 69; Pitroviz: 78, 90, 155; Poleze: 264; Ragnarock: 126 (b); Pepe Ramirez: 31; Tony Robinson: 129; Ronen: 131, 354; ruzanna: 38; Adam J. Sablich: 66; Scott Sanders: 80; Howard Sandler: 23; R. Gino Santa Maria: 278 (t); Slavko Sereda: 41; Vasily Smirnov: 52; Kristin Smith: 127; Perov Stanislav: 365; STILLFX: 30; stocklight: 377; Supri Suharjoto: 81; Svemir: 119; Konstantin Tavrov: 28; TEA: 54 (b); Timurpix: 94; Harald Høiland Tjøstheim: 87; tkemot: 381; Tsian: 125; Ba Tu: 214; Univega: 370; utflytter: 133 (t); Velychko: 76; Wallenrock: 145 (t); Jeff Wilson: 53; Xsandra: 226 (t); Yellowj: 50, 102, 229.

All screengrabs courtesy of the authors and manufacturers.

All other images courtesy of Foundry Arts.